The American Constitution in Context

The American Constitution in Context

BARBARA LAMM

Nova Science Publishers, Inc.
New York

Art Director: Maria Ester Hawrys
Assistant Director: Elenor Kallberg
Graphics: Susan Boriotti and Frank Grucci
Manuscript Coordinator: Phylis Gaynor
Book Production: Gavin Aghamore, Joanne Bennette, Michele Keller, Christine Mathosian and Tammy Sauter
Circulation: Iyatunde Abdullah, Cathy DeGregory and Annette Hellinger

Library of Congress Cataloging–in–Publication Data available upon request

ISBN 1-56072-363-7

6080 Jericho Turnpike, Suite 207
Commack, New York 11725
Tele. 516-499-3103 Fax 516-499-3146
E Mail Novasci1@aol.com

Printed in the United States of America

In Appreciation

My thanks to Barbara and Bob, Willis, Joan, Garna, Duane and everyone else who gave a helping hand with this project.

B.L.

For my son, Willis, and
granddaughter, Cathy
who were the inspiration
for this book.

CONTENTS

Dear Reader,

Why would somebody, at the age of 73, decide to devote the next two years to the development of this book?

Well, I am that somebody and I would like to tell you why I did it.

Concerning the state of the union, sit down as I did one night and say to yourself, *"we have a problem, what can I do about it?"* and see what happens. In my case it led to writing. But that isn't the only way a person can make a meaningful contribution. Our Country is full of constructive ideas anxiously waiting to be developed.

I picked this particular subject because our supreme law of the land, the Constitution, is only able to be as effective as we allow it to be. To have a better understanding of this document can result in it and the country becoming more meaningful in our lives. After all in America we are the government.

Barbara Lamm

Ask not what your country
can do for you - ask what you
can do for your country.

John Fitzgerald Kennedy

35th President (1961-1963)

Assassinated November 22, 1963

Dallas, Texas

Part I

Our Beginning

The Influence of Ancient Rome

The Roman Numeral System

Ancient Romans used capital letters in various combinations instead of numbers as symbols of quantity. Roman numerals 1-1,000, for example, are combinations using seven of our capital letters.

I = 1, V = 5, X = 10, L = 50, C = 100, D = 500, M = 1,000.

The numerals diagrammed here cover those used throughout the United States Constitution.

I	=	1	XVII	=	17 (15+1+1)
II	=	2 (1+1)	XVIII	=	18 (15+1+1+1)
III	=	3 (1+1+1)	XIX	=	19 (20-1)
IV	=	4 (5-1)	XX	=	20 (20)
V	=	5 (5)	XXI	=	21 (20+1)
VI	=	6 (5+1)	XXII	=	22 (20+1+1)
VII	=	7 (5+1+1)	XXIII	=	23 (20+1+1+1)
VIII	=	8 (5+1+1+1)	XXIV	=	24 (25-1)
IX	=	9 (10-1)	XXV	=	25 (25)
X	=	10 (10)	XXVI	=	26 (25+1)

XI	=	11 (10+1)	XXVII	=	27 (25+1+1)
XII	=	12 (10+1+1)	XXVIII	=	28 (25+1+1+1)
XIII	=	13 (10+1+1+1)	XXIX	=	29 (30-1)
XIV	=	14 (15-1)	XXX	=	30 (30)
XV	=	15 (15)	XL	=	40 (50-10)
XVI	=	16 (15+1)	L	=	50 (50)

Roman Architecture

The Roman Empire was so vast, incredibly advanced, and well organized (until its last days) that it has made a lasting impression on the Western World in every area. Our national Capitol, the White House and other federal buildings, as well as structures throughout the country, were inspired by Ancient Rome, particularly in the early days of our development.

Roman Sculpture

Horatio Greenough's startling statue of a seated George Washington, draped and posed like an ancient god, was originally viewed in the rotunda of the U.S. Capitol. Because of its massive weight, 20 tons of solid marble, it was making the floor sag and had to be moved outside. Eventually, it reached the safer custody of the Smithsonian Institution.

This statue of George Washington was patterned after the all-knowing and all-seeing Greek god Zeus, whose Roman equivalent was Jupiter.

Roman Language

Many roots of our language and others come from Latin, the language of Ancient Rome. We still use pure Latin words and phrases such as our national motto, E PLURIBUS UNUM, meaning "One Out of Many." The Latin legal phrases referred to in the Constitution - *pro tempore, habeas corpus and ex post facto* - will be discussed later. (See *The Constitution and The People.*)

Landmark Events Leading to the Constitution

THE REVOLUTIONARY MOVEMENT OF THE UNITED COLONIES 1763 - 1773

This was the period in which colonial grievances against King George III accelerated to the point that 13 of the British colonies banned together to forcefully express their displeasure.

Florida was also a British colony at this time, in sympathy with the others, but not ready to join their movement.

THE FIRST CONTINENTAL CONGRESS SEPTEMBER AND OCTOBER, 1774

Every colony sent delegates to this Congress except Georgia. Massachusetts was represented by Bill and John Adams; Virginia, by George Washington and Patrick Henry. At this stage the colonies called themselves "The United Colonies." They still hoped for reconciliation, but suggested that all colonies cut off trade with Britain if matters failed to improve and begin training civilians for a possible serious conflict. A tentative date was set for a second meeting.

The Second Continental Congress May, 1775

Fighting had begun in April at Lexington and Concord in Massachusetts. In this meeting the Continental Army was formed under George Washington and strategy developed for conducting the Revolution. Representatives from the colonies changed from time to time, but the Second Continental Congress functioned as our central government until the Articles of Confederation were adopted in 1781 - two years before the end of the American Revolution.

The Committee on the Declaration of Independence

By June of 1776 all colonies agreed that it was time to establish in writing why they were fighting for their independence, so that Great Britain and all the world would know, and support from some other countries might be forthcoming. The committee of the Second Continental Congress chosen to create this document included Chairman Thomas Jefferson (VA), John Adams (MA), Roger Sherman (CT), Benjamin Franklin (PA) and Robert Livingston (NY). Jefferson was given credit for most of the writing.

In the Declaration the colonists directed their anger primarily against King George III. Great Britain was an advanced nation for the times. The power of their monarchy was not absolute. The colonists had respect for the British legal system and incorporated parts of it in the Constitution. It had been hoped that the British Parliament could temper the king's actions, but the conflict had become too bitter for any kind of reconciliation.

Jefferson went so far as to accuse the king of having introduced slavery in America. That paragraph was deleted from the final draft. (It was the Dutch who introduced the African slave trade.) Most colonists realized that to make an issue of slavery at that time would destroy the cohesion necessary for them to win and sustain independence. They had dared to have a showdown with a major European power that had successfully cleared the area of all foreign intervention.

It is important to remember that had we lost the American Revolution our colonial leaders would have been shipped to England in chains and hanged as traitors, And they knew it.

The Declaration of Independence is presented here in its entirety because it so ably expressed the colonial heartbeat of the Revolution that was ultimately reflected in the U.S. Constitution. It does need to be pointed out that in the Constitution the key to human rights, referred to in this document as "unalienable Rights", is *citizenship*. The importance of citizenship in relation to the law was an Ancient Roman concept not lost on the colonies. The benefits of the legal system under the U.S. Constitution were to be for all citizens of the United States of America. The issue of slavery was left in the hands of the states.

THE DECLARATION OF INDEPENDENCE JULY 4, 1776

(A declaration of intent to achieve independence)

When in the Course of human events, it becomes necessary for one people to dissolve the political bands which have connected them with another, and to assume among the powers of the earth, the separate and equal station to which the Laws of Nature and of Nature's God entitle them, a decent respect to the opinions of mankind requires that they should declare the causes which impel them to the separation.

(Our philosophy of government established)

We hold these truths to be self-evident, that all men are created equal, that they are endowed by their Creator with certain unalienable Rights, that among these are Life, Liberty, and the pursuit of Happiness. That to secure these rights, Governments are instituted among Men, deriving their just powers from the consent of the governed, That whenever any Form of Government becomes destructive of these ends, it is the Right of the People to alter or to abolish it, and to institute new Government, laying its foundation on such principles and organizing its powers in such form, as to them shall seem most likely to effect their Safety and Happiness. Prudence, indeed, will dictate that Governments long established should not be changed for light and transient causes; and accordingly all experience hath shown, that mankind are more disposed to suffer, while evils are sufferable, than to right themselves by abolishing the forms to which they are accustomed. But when a long train of abuses and usurpations, pursuing invariably the same Object evinces a design to reduce them under absolute Despotism, it is their right, it is their duty, to throw off such Government, and to provide new Guards for their future security. Such has been the patient sufferance of these Colonies; and such is now the necessity which constrains them to alter their former Systems of Government. The history of the present King of Great Britain is a history of repeated injuries and usurpations, all having in direct object the establishment of an absolute Tyranny over these States.

(Grievances against King George III)

To prove this, let Facts be submitted to a candid world.

He has refused his Assent to Laws, the most wholesome and necessary for the public good.

He has forbidden his Governors to pass Laws of immediate and pressing importance, unless suspended in their operation till his Assent should be obtained; and when so suspended, he has utterly neglected to attend to them.

He has refused to pass other Laws for the accommodation of large districts of people, unless those people would relinquish the right of Representation in the Legislature, a right inestimable to them and formidable to tyrants only.

He has called together legislative bodies at places unusual, uncomfortable, and distant from the depository of their public Records, for the sole purpose of fatiguing them into compliance with his measures.

He has dissolved Representative Houses repeatedly, for opposing with manly firmness his invasions on the rights of the people.

He has refused for a long time, after such dissolutions, to cause others to be elected; whereby the Legislative powers, incapable of Annihilation, have returned to the People at large for their exercise; the State remaining in the meantime exposed to all the dangers of invasion from without, and convulsions within.

He has endeavored to prevent the population of these States; for that purpose obstructing the Laws for Naturalization of Foreigners; refusing to pass others to encourage their migration hither, and raising the conditions of new Appropriations of Lands.

He has obstructed the Administration of Justice, by refusing his Assent to Laws for establishing Judiciary powers.

He has made Judges dependent on his Will alone, for the tenure of their offices, and the amount and payment of their salaries.

He has erected a multitude of New Offices, and sent hither swarms of Officers to harass our people, and eat out their substance.

He has kept among us, in times of peace, Standing Armies, without the Consent of our legislatures.

He has affected to render the Military independent of and superior to the Civil power.

He has combined with others to subject us to a jurisdiction foreign to our constitution, and unacknowledged by our laws; giving his Assent to their Acts of pretended Legislation:

For quartering large bodies of armed troops among us:

For protecting them, by a mock Trial, from punishment for any Murders which they should commit on the Inhabitants of these States:

For cutting off our Trade with all parts of the world:

For imposing Taxes on us without our Consent:

For depriving us in many cases, of the benefits of Trial by Jury:

For transporting us beyond Seas to be tried for pretended offenses:

For abolishing the free System of English Laws in a neighboring Province, establishing therein an Arbitrary government, and enlarging its Boundaries so as to render it at once an example and fit instrument for introducing the same absolute rule into these Colonies:

For taking away our Charters, abolishing our most valuable Laws, and altering fundamentally the Forms of our Governments:

For suspending our own Legislatures, and declaring themselves invested with power to legislate for us in all cases whatsoever.

He has abdicated Government here, by declaring us out of his Protection and waging War against us.

He has plundered our seas, ravaged our Coasts, burnt our towns, and destroyed the lives of our people.

He is at this time transporting large Armies of foreign Mercenaries to compleat the works of death, desolation and tyranny, already begun with circumstances of Cruelty & perfidy scarcely paralleled in the most barbarous ages, and totally unworthy the Head of a civilized nation.

He has constrained our fellow Citizens taken Captive on the high Seas to bear Arms against their Country, to become the executioners of their friends and Brethren, or to fall themselves by their Hands.

He has excited domestic insurrections amongst us, and has endeavoured to bring on the inhabitants of our frontiers, the merciless Indian Savages, whose known rule of warfare, is an undistinguished destruction of all ages, sexes and conditions.

In every stage of these Oppressions We have Petitioned for Redress in the most humble terms: Our repeated Petitions have been answered only by repeated injury. A Prince, whose character is thus marked by every act which may define a Tyrant, is unfit to be the ruler of a free people.

Nor have We been wanting in attentions to our British brethren. We have warned them from time to time of attempts by their legislature to extend an unwarrantable jurisdiction over us. We have reminded them of the circumstances of our emigration and settlement here. We have appealed to their native justice and magnanimity, and we have conjured them by the ties of our common kindred to disavow these usurpations, which, would inevitably interrupt our connections and correspondence. They too have been deaf to the voice of justice and of consanguinity. We must, therefore, acquiesce in the necessity, which denounces our Separation, and hold them, as we hold the rest of mankind, Enemies in War, in Peace Friends.

(Emergence of the United States of America)

We, THEREFORE, THE REPRESENTATIVES OF THE UNITED STATES OF AMERICA, in General Congress, Assembled, appealing to the Supreme Judge of the world for the rectitude of our intentions, do, in

the Name, and by Authority of the good People of these Colonies, solemnly publish and declare, That these United Colonies are, and of Right ought to be FREE AND INDEPENDENT STATES; that they are Absolved from all
Allegiance to the British Crown, and that all political connection between them and the State of Great Britain, is and ought to be totally dissolved; and that as Free and Independent States, they have full Power to levy War, conclude Peace, contract Alliances, establish Commerce, and to do all other Acts and Things which Independent States may of right do. And for the support of this Declaration, with a firm reliance on the protection of Divine Providence, we mutually pledge to each other our Lives, our Fortunes and our sacred Honor.

John Hancock

NOTE: Following the signature of John Hancock are the signatures of representatives from all 13 colonies, hereafter known as the United States of America.

THE ARTICLES OF CONFEDERATION OF THE UNITED STATES 1781 - 1789

It is not surprising that very few changes were made in the Articles. The Continental Congress had successfully assumed whatever powers were deemed necessary to carry on the war and at this time no state was willing to wear the yoke provided by a strong central government. More than anything else the Articles gave legitimacy to the governing powers of the Continental Congress.

There was a simple one-chamber Congress with each state having one vote. Any action required the approval of nine states; and an amendment, the approval of all the states. No executive branch (President) or judicial branch (Supreme Court) was incorporated. The states had total authority and authorized their Congress to:

1. determine war and peace and make treaties
2. establish on army and navy and appoint the high ranking military officers
3. decide certain kinds of disputes among the states and create courts to try such things
4. as piracies and felonies
5. distribute any bounty received among the states
6. send and receive ambassadors and, in general, manage foreign affairs
7. regulate Indian affairs
8. issue, borrow and regulate the value of money and issue bills of credit
9. fix standards of weights and measures
10. establish a postal system

There were some serious weaknesses in congressional authority under the Articles. Congress had no commerce power or authorization to tax individuals. All of the money had to be supplied by the states. Also Congress was lacking in really effective means of enforcing any regulations a state chose to ignore or dispute. The United States was functioning more like a league of city-states than a nation.

After the flush of victory when the American Revolution ended in 1783, the states began to take stock of their internal weaknesses, Indian problems, and the strength of foreign powers that still controlled most of the country. The Constitutional Convention was finally called to review the Articles of Confederation and see what changes should be made. It was generally believed that an entirely new form of government would not be necessary.

Virginia thought otherwise.

THE CONSTITUTIONAL CONVENTION

MAY - SEPTEMBER, 1787

> We are sent here to consult --- harmony and union are extremely necessary to give weight to our councils and render them effectual in promoting and securing the common good.
>
> Benjamin Franklin

FIRST DAYS

Of the 74 delegates appointed by their states, 55 attended the Convention. It was like Oscar night in Hollywood with some of the finest revolutionary minds in attendance: Virginia's George Washington, unanimously elected convention president, with Edmund Randolph and James Madison, called the "Father of the Constitution" because of his meticulous record keeping of all Convention events; the senior member, Benjamin Franklin, with Gouverneur Morris and the Scottish born and educated lawyer, James Wilson, of the Pennsylvania team; Alexander Hamilton, New York's representative, whose biggest job would be to get his state to ratify; South Carolina's cousins Charles Pinckney and Charles Cotesworth Pinckney, prominent planters and political leaders; and Roger Sherman, a strong voice from Connecticut. Luther Martin of Maryland and George Mason of Virginia refrained from signing the Constitution because they believed it gave too much power to the central government. Mason, who also opposed slavery, had written Virginia's Declaration of Rights in 1776. *(See Profiles of the 13 Original States* - Virginia.*)*

NOTABLY ABSENT

There were no delegates from the state of Rhode Island. Thomas Jefferson and John Adams were on government business in Europe; Thomas Paine had returned to England; Patrick Henry was not in favor of changing the

Articles; Samuel Adams and John Hancock had not been chosen this time to represent their state of Massachusetts.

A Cross Section of Signers of the Constitution

Abraham Baldwin - Georgia Delegate

Connecticut born graduate of Yale College; minister and tutor at Yale; army chaplain in the Revolution; after the war turned to the legal profession and later helped establish Georgia's educational system; represented that state in the U.S. House of Representatives and Senate.

John Blair - Virginia Delegate

State legislator, lawyer and judge; attended the College of William and Mary and studied law in London, England; on the committee that drafted Virginia's first Constitution; became an associate justice (appointed by President Washington) on the first U.S. Supreme Court. Favored a strong central government.

William Blount - North Carolina Delegate

Paymaster for NC troops in the Revolution; instrumental in getting the Constitution ratified in North Carolina. When George Washington became president, was appointed the first territorial governor of Tennessee.

Jacob Broom - Delaware Delegate

Farmer, state legislator, businessman; occupational endeavors included banking, surveying, shipping and the manufacture and repair of machinery. A cotton factory that he owned was one of the first of its kind in the country. He was also the first postmaster in the city of Wilmington.

Pierce Butler - South Carolina Delegate

Wealthy planter and statesman; born in county Carlow, Ireland; Father, Richard, a member of the Irish Parliament. Originally came to South Carolina as a major in the British Army; married the daughter of a prominent planter and remained in this country. Favored a strong central government.

Jonathan Dayton - New Jersey Delegate

Business investor, political leader. At the age of 26, the youngest signer of the Constitution. A graduate of the College of New Jersey when only 16 years old; an army captain in the Revolution. Charged with high treason in 1807 concerning western political schemes with Aaron Burr, but the case never went to trial. Looked for land investments in Ohio and had the city of Dayton, Ohio named after him. For strong states' rights.

Alexander Hamilton - New York Delegate

Lawyer, statesman, political leader; born on the island of Nevis in the West Indies; son of a Scottish merchant. Graduate of what today is known as Columbia University. Captain of a NY artillery company in the Revolution and assistant to General Washington. Favored a strong central government. Hamilton was shot and killed in a duel called by Aaron Burr on July 11, 1804. He was accused by Burr of slander and obstruction of Burr's campaign to become governor of New York. Hamilton had previously worked against Burr becoming president of the United States. (Burr was chosen by the Electoral College to become vice president in the Jefferson Administration.)

Rufus King - Massachusetts Delegate

Statesman and diplomat; born in Scarboro, Maine, at that time a part of Massachusetts; friend of Alexander Hamilton; noted for his opposition to the expansion of slavery in the West; in later years a minister to Great Britain and presidential candidate.

John Langdon - New Hampshire Delegate

Ship captain and merchant who built ships for the Continental Navy in the Revolution; represented New Hampshire in the Second Continental Congress; became a U.S. senator and, ultimately, state governor. An advocate of strong central government.

James McHenry - Maryland Delegate

Doctor and politician; born in Ballymena, Ireland; army surgeon and secretary to Generals Washington and the Marquis de Lafayette during the Revolution; helped shape the final draft of the U.S. Constitution. Became the first Secretary of War.

Governeur Morris - Pennsylvania Delegate

Statesman and diplomat who headed the committee that wrote the final draft of the Constitution; later minister to France and a U.S. senator from New York where he was born. Lost his left leg in his youth in a carriage accident and spent his vigorous adult life with one peg leg. Favored a strong central government.

Robert Morris - Pennsylvania Delegate

Born near Liverpool, England. Came to America at the age of 13; valuable member of a shipping and banking firm by the time he was 20; served in the Second Continental Congress. Called the "Financier of the American Revolution" because of his ability to raise large sums of money for the Continental Army.

Roger Sherman - Connecticut Delegate

Judge, businessman, political leader. The only person to have signed the Articles of Association (1774), the Declaration of Independence (1776), Articles of Confederation (1777) and U.S. Constitution (1787); presented the Connecticut Compromise at the Constitutional Convention. His statue represents the state of Connecticut in the U.S. Capitol in Washington.

Important Convention Events

The Virginia Plan

In the lull of the first days while delegates waited for all attending members to arrive, the Virginia representatives went into a huddle and came out with a new government. As soon as the opening formalities were over Edmund Randolph took the floor and presented Virginia's fifteen resolutions, which were a dramatic departure from the existing framework. When the stunned delegates recovered, their attention was so centered on the pros and cons of the Virginia Plan that the Articles of Confederation were virtually forgotten.

The New Jersey Plan

Fearful that the small states would be left behind, New Jersey formed a plan of nine resolutions which were introduced by their representative William Paterson.

The Last Days

In the end most of the original Virginia Plan was combined with Connecticut's compromise which it was decided presented the best balance for all states concerned.

CONSTITUTIONAL REFERENCE

Article VII, Par. (2)

DONE in Convention by the Unanimous Consent of the States present the Seventeenth Day of September in the Year of our Lord one thousand seven hundred and Eighty seven and of the Independence of the United States of America the Twelfth In witness whereof We have hereunto subscribed our Names, attest William Jackson Secretary

G. Washington - Presidt
and deputy from Virginia

In **Article VII, Par. (2)**, the quotation "--- the United States of America the Twelfth," relates to the fact that 12 of the 13 United States were present to create and approve this document. The statement did not disqualify the 13th state, Rhode Island, from ratifying the Constitution.

On September 17, 1787 one of the most important political documents in history was completed. With the ratification of the ninth state, New Hampshire, on June 21, 1788, it became the law of the United States of America. The four states that had not yet ratified - Virginia, New York, North Carolina and Rhode Island - complied in that order by May of 1790.

> I have lived a long time, and the longer I live, the more convincing proofs I see of this truth - that God governs in the affairs of men.
>
> Benjamin Franklin
> 1706-1790

Profiles of the 13 Original States

Key Words and Phrases

Algonquin; Algonquian
Algonquin is the name of an Indian tribe; The Algonquian language family or group refers to all tribes that speak this language. This pattern also applies to other Indian language groups, such as Iroquoian (Iroquois) and Siouan (Sioux).

charter
a document from a ruler or government that grants certain rights or defines the form an institution should take.

commonwealth
an independent nation, state or community.

Minutemen
revolutionary civilians trained to fight on a minute's notice.

Mound Builders
ancient Indians who created such lasting earth structures as temple foundations, burials and dwellings for tribal chiefs.

to ratify; ratification
to agree, confirm; an agreement having legal force.
sovereign state

an independent state with governing powers; the USA is a union of sovereign states.

CONSTITUTIONAL REFERENCE

Article VII, Par. (1) - Ratification of the Constitution:

The Ratification of the Conventions of nine States, shall be sufficient for the Establishment of this Constitution between the States so ratifying the Same.

NOTE: All of the states - some unanimously, some by a narrow margin - ratified between December, 1787 and May, 1790. At the time the Constitution was ratified the 13 states included territory that would later become the states of Kentucky, Maine, Tennessee, Vermont and West Virginia, which will be discussed in this chapter.

THE 13 ORIGINAL STATES

Profiles of the 13 original states include state names and official abbreviations, ratification dates and delegates who signed the Constitution. In the Constitution delegate signatures follow **Article VII, Par. (2)** in the body of the document.

CONNECTICUT (CT) - 5th state to ratify, January 9, 1788.

Delegates: William Samuel Johnson and Roger Sherman.

Early Settlers: Several tribes of the Algonquian Indian family, the Pequot being the most powerful, lived in this area. The Mohican (Mahican) were the subject of the American writer, James Fenimore Cooper, in his book "The Last of the Mohicans." Another tribe, the Mohegan, were related to the Pequot Indians and fought with the colonists against the British.

European Settlers: Dutch claims were taken over by the British. (See Delaware.)

USA: The development of the two-house Congress in the Constitution was designed by Connecticut to arrive at balanced representation of the states in our central government. The Connecticut Compromise is usually referred to as the Great Compromise. The American Revolution was enhanced by the availability of Connecticut's ports, iron furnaces and forges, and large numbers of volunteers for the Continental Army.

DELAWARE (DE) - 1st state to ratify, December 7, 1787.

Delegates: George Read, Gunning Bedford Jr., John Dickinson, Richard Bassett and Jacob Broom.

Early Settlers: The Lenni-Lenape (a tribe of the Delaware) and Nanticoke of the Algonquian family were the most numerous Indians.

European Settlers: The first permanent settlement (1638), on the border of the Pennsylvania/Delaware territory near Philadelphia, was named New Sweden. It was the only Swedish settlement ever attempted and was seized by the Dutch in 1655. Dutch New Netherland included parts of Delaware, New Jersey, and New York, and trading posts in Pennsylvania and Connecticut. At this time Europeans had little understanding of the size and complexity of America, and the British, who believed their eastern claims to be the original ones extending from ocean to ocean, felt justified in driving out the Dutch. Delaware functioned under Pennsylvania governors until the American Revolution.

USA: Delaware declared independence from Great Britain at the Second Continental Congress and was active in the Revolution even though only one battle was fought on Delaware soil.

GEORGIA (GA) - 4th state to ratify, January 2, 1788.

Delegates: William Few and Abraham Baldwin.

Early Settlers: Ancient Mound Builders were ancestors of such tribes as the Creek and Cherokee Indians.

European Settlers: The Spanish were later replaced by British whose plan was to make the region a haven for debtors, but few came. The first settlers arrived in 1733 with the Englishman, James Oglethorpe and a 21-year charter. The colony was named Georgia for King George II. Friendly Creek Indians allowed them to live in peace. Georgia was made a royal province in 1754.

USA: The British seized much of this region early in the Revolution and Georgia troops spent most of the war driving them out.

Liberation: Georgia was the first state to grant women property rights and implement the **26th Amendment**, the right of 18-year-olds to vote. African-American civil rights leader, Julian Bond, was in the Georgia House of Representatives from 1965 - 1975 and the state Senate, 1975-1987.

MARYLAND (MD) - 7th state to ratify, April 28, 1788.

Delegates: James McHenry, Daniel Jenifer of St. Thomas and Daniel Carroll.

Early Settlers: Ancient Indians lived in this region. Explorers found a few Susquehannock and Nanticoke among the scattered tribes.

European Settlers: Spanish were followed by British. The second Lord Baltimore of England was granted a charter for this territory in 1632 by King Charles I, which he named Maryland in honor of the king's wife, Maria. Maryland passed a religious tolerance act in 1649.

USA: After attending the First and Second Continental Congress Maryland voted for independence and served with distinction in the Revolution.

Flying the Flag: Baltimore's Fort McHenry, which withstood heavy British bombardment in the War of 1812, inspired Francis Scott Key to write "The Star-Spangled Banner."

MASSACHUSETTS (MA) - 6th state to ratify, February 6, 1788.

Delegates: Nathaniel Gorham and Rufus King.

Early Setters: This area was primarily settled by Indians of the Algonquian Family - the Pennacook and Wampanoag. Disease took many even before Europeans arrived.

European Settlers: It is believed Vikings first sighted the coast followed by Spanish and French, but it remained for the British to be the settlers. Pilgrims, known as Separatists, broke from the Church of England and in the *Mayflower* left Plymouth, England reaching what is now called Provincetown harbor in November, 1620. Local Indians helped them survive the winter. The Puritans, 10 years later, received a charter from King Charles I of England to form the Massachusetts Bay Colony near Boston. Some took root in Salem. The Bay Colony championed religious freedom and representative government, but the Puritans refused to allow other than their own faith to flourish.

USA: It was in this state that the American Revolution began. Massachusetts produced Henry Knox, our first Secretary of War, and John Adams, who became our first Vice President and second President of the United States.

NEW HAMPSHIRE (NH) - 9th state to ratify, June 21, 1788.

This ratification made the U.S. Constitution the law of the land.

Delegates: John Langdon and Nicholas Gilman.

Early Settlers: The most prominent Indian tribes were the Abenaki and Pennacook of the Algonquian Family. They were brought close to destruction by European settlers and their Indian adversaries, the Mohawk.

European Settlers: France lost this region and practically all holdings east of the Mississippi River in the French and Indian Wars (1689-1763). This periodic conflict between France and Great Britain (with Spain an ally of France and Indians on both sides) was the last important conflict before the American Revolution.

USA: This was the only state in which no fighting took place in the Revolution. New Hampshire's Minutemen joined Massachusetts forces.

A Melting Pot: New Hampshire's first settlers were primarily Scotch-Irish. Later arrivals came from all parts of Europe and particularly from the French Quebec province of Canada.

NEW JERSEY (NJ) - 3rd state to ratify, December 18, 1787.

Delegates: William Livingston, David Brearley, William Paterson and Jonathan Dayton.

Early Settlers: The Delaware tribe, the Lenni-Lenape (meaning "genuine people"), appear to have been the earliest settlers.

European Settlers: There were Italian and British explorations, but the Dutch and some Swedes were the first white settlers. Final control was won by the British. (See Delaware.) The eastern part of the region was noted for its religious tolerance.

USA: At the end of the American Revolution, the New Jersey cities of Princeton, in 1783 and Trenton, in 1784 were our national capital. Many battles were fought in this state, partly because of its strategic location between Philadelphia, PA and New York City.

A Big Dig: The first dinosaur skeleton ever discovered in North America was found in Haddonfield, NJ, in 1858.

NEW YORK (NY) - 11th state to ratify, July 26, 1788.

Delegate: Alexander Hamilton.

Early Settlers: Two powerful Indian adversaries dominated this region: the Iroquois nations - Onondaga, Seneca, Cayuga, Oneida and Mohawk - of the Iroquois Confederacy, verses the Delaware, Mohegan, Montauk and Munsee (a division of the Delaware) of the Algonquian Family. The Montauk were extinct by the late 1800's.

European Settlers: The Dutch gained control of what is now known as Manhattan Island (New York City) by purchasing it from the Indians in goods worth about $24. They named it New Amsterdam. Then in 1664 the British sailed in with guns bristling and the Dutch withdrew without a shot being fired. (See Delaware.) The territory was renamed New York for the English Duke of York who later became King James II.

USA: George Washington on April 30, 1789 took the Oath of Office as our first president in New York City, the U.S. capital from 1785 to 1790. Washington appointed New York's Alexander Hamilton Secretary of the Treasury, and John Jay, the first Chief Justice of the Supreme Court.

NORTH CAROLINA (NC) - 12th state to ratify, November 21, 1789.

Delegates: William Blount, Richard Dobbs Spaight and Hugh Williamson.

Early Settlers: Among the leading Indian tribes were the Cherokee, Catawba and Tuscarora.

European Settlers: There were French and Spanish explorations before the first British settlement organized by Sir Walter Raleigh in 1585 on Roanoke Island, NC. This discouraged group went back to England and was replaced by another under John White in 1587. Three years later, when White returned to America after a trip to England for supplies, he was unable to find a trace of his colony of over 100 men, women and children. The fate of what has become known as The Lost Colony has never been determined. It wasn't until around 1650 that this region gained permanent settlements when colonists from Virginia began to arrive. North Carolina, separated from South Carolina by 1712, was made a royal colony in 1729.

USA: Little fighting took place in the Revolution in this state, but many NC troops joined forces with VA troops where the conflict was more intense.

PENNSYLVANIA (PA) - 2nd state to ratify, December 12, 1787.

Delegates: Benjamin Franklin, Thomas Mifflin, Robert Morris, George Clymer, Thomas FitzSimons, Jared Ingersoll, James Wilson and Gouverneur Morris.

Early Settlers: Ancient Indians were followed by Shawnee, Delaware, Nanticoke and Conoy (Algonquian), and the Susquehannock of the Iroquois Family.

European Settlers: British drove out the Dutch in 1664. (See Delaware.) King Charles II granted the territory to William Penn and his Quaker followers who reached their destination in 1682. Penn named the region Sylvania (meaning "woods"), but the King added Penn in honor of William's father who was an English admiral. Penn achieved a treaty of friendship with the local Indians and paid them for most of the land his colony occupied.

USA: Philadelphia was the site of the First and Second Continental Congress, the Declaration of Independence and the Constitutional Convention.

RHODE ISLAND (RI) - 13th state to ratify, May 29, 1790.

Delegates: None. Rhode Island adopted a wait-and-see attitude.

Early Settlers: Members of the Algonquian Indian Family, the Narragansett being the most numerous, dominated this area. Others included the Niantic, Pequot and Wampanoag.

European Settlers: The Englishman, Roger Williams, left Massachusetts and formed the first permanent white settlement in Providence, RI in

1636. He bought his land from two Narragansett Indian Chiefs and established a policy of religious and political freedom. Rhode Island's burning of the British ship, the *Liberty* in 1769 was one of the first colonial acts of defiance against the British.

USA: Rhode Island was the first colony to declare independence (May, 1776) and was active in the Revolution.

Item of Note: Much of Providence is as it was in the 1700's. The Providence Unitarian Church is in possession of the largest bell ever cast by Paul Revere's foundry.

SOUTH CAROLINA (SC) - 8th state to ratify, May 23, 1788.

Delegates: John Rutledge, Charles Cotesworth Pinckney, Charles Pinckney and Pierce Butler.

Early Settlers: Here some of the leading Indian tribes were the Catawba, Cherokee and Yamasee.

European Settlers: Spanish explored, but it was eight English noblemen called lords proprietors who in 1670 colonized the Carolinas under a charter from King Charles II. North and South Carolina developed separate governors by 1712. In 1719, to the relief of the unhappy colonists who chafed under the proprietors, King George I made this region a royal province. South Carolina became Britain's southern line of defense against the French and Spanish.

USA: Bands of South Carolinians such as the one under the "Swamp Fox," General Francis Marion, constantly harassed the British during the Revolution.

Acting It Out: Charleston's Dock Theater was the first building in America specifically built for dramatic stage productions.

VIRGINIA (VA) - 10th state to ratify, June 25, 1788.

Delegates: John Blair and James Madison, Jr. As president of the Constitutional Convention, George Washington placed his signature at the end of the document, not with the other signers.

Early Settlers: Members of three different Indian language groups occupied this region: The Cherokee and Nottoway of the Iroquoian language; Powhatan of the Algonquian; and Monacan, Ocaneechi, Manahoac and Nahyssan of the Siouan group. The Monacan lost their identity in the colonial period and the Nottoway became extinct in the early 1800's.

European Settlers: The Virginia Company of London in 1607, under Captain John Smith, founded the first colony called Jamestown in honor of England's King James I. This charter was revoked and Virginia made a royal colony in 1624.

The Virginia Commonwealth: By 1776 Virginia had become an independent commonwealth and developed the first bill of rights in an American constitution, which became known as the Declaration of Rights.

USA: Of the first five presidents of the United States, four were from Virginia. (See *The President.*)

STATES FORMED FROM THE ORIGINAL 13

Constitutional Reference

Summary of Article IV, Sec. 3, Par. (1) - New States:

New states may be admitted by Congress alone into this Union, but Congress must also have the consent of the legislatures of all states concerned involving the creation of a new state out of one or more of the existing states.

KENTUCKY (KY) - 15th state, June 1, 1792.

Early Settlers: In this area Indians go back about 15,000 years, primarily in the forests. Explorers found Chickasaw, Shawnee, Cherokee, Delaware and Wyandot.

USA: Scouts claimed this region for the United States. Kentucky's first white settlement was established at Harrodsburg by John Harrod of Pennsylvania in 1774, and Daniel Boone's Boonesborough developed along the Kentucky River. Our 16th president, Abraham Lincoln, was born near Hodgenville. Kentucky was made a county of Virginia in 1776. By 1792, two years after all of the original states had ratified the Constitution, Kentucky settled boundary disputes with Virginia and petitioned Congress for statehood.

Racy News: The annual Kentucky Derby horse race at Churchill Downs in Louisville began in 1875 and has been an international winner ever since.

MAINE (ME) - 23rd state, March 15, 1820.

Early Settlers: The Abenaki and Etchemin of the Algonquian Family dominated this region, but were frequently challenged by Iroquois. The Etchemin, a smaller tribe than the Abenaki, became extinct in the colonial days.

European Settlers: Vikings, then the French explored the Maine coast. They were followed by the Venetian, John Cabot, in the service of England in 1498. Both Spanish and Portuguese probed for gold and a northwest passage to the Orient. A British settlement in the early 1600's did not last, but does get credit for being the first British colony to build a boat, which was named the *Virginia.*

USA: Maine functioned as part of Massachusetts from 1677 to 1819 when the people of that region voted for independence and statehood.

Ship Ahoy!: In 1803 Commodore Edward Preble led a successful expedition against the Barbary Coast pirates. Maine's maritime contributions go back to the first naval battle of the American Revolution.

TENNESSEE (TN) - 16th state, June 1, 1796.

Early Settlers: Ancestors of the Cherokee and Chickasaw Indians built mounds. Shawnee occupied the middle of the state.

European Settlers: The British made the Tennessee region a part of the colony of North Carolina.

USA: In 1789 North Carolina gave the territory of Tennessee to the federal government. After Tennessee became a state, the Chickasaw Indians (1818) sold their holdings east of the Mississippi River to the federal government, which included what is today the western part of Tennessee.

Tall Tales Territory: The Tennessee wilderness produced the kind of men legends were made of - "Davy" Crockett, David Farragut, Nathan Forrest and John Sevier. In the American Revolution it was reported that Sevier and his followers, using Indian tactics, wiped out about half of a British Force of over 1,000 soldiers with a loss of only 28 of his own men. Tales don't come taller than that in Texas.

VERMONT (VT) - 14th state, March 4, 1791.

Early Settlers: This was chiefly an Indian hunting ground. Continuous conflict resulted between the Algonquian tribes - Mohegan, Abenaki and Pennacook - and their Iroquois opponents.

European Settlers: Great Britain gained the territory of Vermont at the end of the French and Indian Wars. (See New Hampshire.)

The Republic: In 1777 Vermont took action and declared itself the Republic of New Connecticut. The name was later changed to Vermont. During the 14 years as a republic Vermont settled a border dispute with New Hampshire and paid New York $30,000 for that state's land claims. While still a republic, Vermont supported the colonies in the American Revolution.

USA: Vermont was made our 14th state three years after the Constitution became law.

For Good Measure: Steel carpenter squares, originally invented in Vermont, were still being manufactured in the last half of this century by the same company that began making them in the early 1800's.

WEST VIRGINIA (WV) - 35th state, June 20, 1863.

Early Settlers: Prehistoric Indians were Mound Builders. Later there were Cherokee, Iroquois and Shawnee who depleted their ranks fighting over hunting grounds before the conflict with white settlers began.

European Settlers: Settlements included many Germans and Scotch- Irish. This area was made a part of the British colony of Virginia, but the two sections were never very compatible.

USA: The Battle of Point Pleasant in 1774, which took place in western Virginia, is considered by some historians to be the beginning of the American Revolution.

Statehood: In the Civil War, after Virginia joined the Confederacy, the western part of the state petitioned Congress to remain in the Union and become the state of West Virginia.

Settling Up: The U.S. Supreme Court in *Virginia v West Virginia (1915)* ruled that West Virginia owed Virginia over $12 million - part of the state debt at the time the two sections of Virginia separated. West Virginia made final payment in 1939.

Odds and Ends

When Did Our Oldest Become Our Newest Amendment?

This Amendment, prohibiting Congress from granting itself any mid-term salary increases except at election time, was proposed by James Madison and submitted by Congress to the states on September 25, 1789, two years after the signing of the Constitution. It became the law when Michigan, the 38th state, ratified in May 7, 1992 - *203 years later*! In this period we had grown from 13 to 50 states and added 26 amendments to the Constitution.

Congress did not originally place a time limit on this amendment, the usual allowance being seven years, but could have declared it invalid after such a long period of time. However, it has been made our **27th Amendment.**

NOTE: The **27th Amendment** was originally a part of 12 amendments that were proposed in 1789. Of these, 10 were ratified on December 15, 1791 and became known as the Bill of Rights.

Washington, DC - The District of Columbia

Key Words and Phrases

to annex; annexation

to act, join to a larger thing; the act of acquiring new territory.

to cede; cession

to yield, formally surrender or make over; the act of giving up one's right to something such as territory.

elector; Electoral College

a person who has the power to vote in an election; the Electoral College is the body of electors chosen by their states to vote for the President and Vice President of the United States.

home rule

degree of self government.

jurisdiction

authority to interpret and apply the law; the extent or territory over which legal or other power extends.

Constitutional References

Summary of Article I, Sec. 8, Par. (17)
Congressional Authority Over Lands for Public Use

Congress has exclusive authority over a district, not to exceed 10 square miles, ceded to the government by a state and accepted by Congress to become the United States seat of government. Congress has the same authority over land purchased, with the consent of the legislatures of the states involved, for the erection of dock-yards, arsenals and other facilities needed for public use.

Summary of the 23rd Amendment (1961)
DC Voting Rights in National Elections

"The District constituting the seat of Government of the United States shall appoint in such manner as the Congress may direct:" electors for the purpose of voting in national elections for the President and Vice President of the United States. The district is allotted as many electors as the state with the least number.

NOTE: Since Wyoming, the state with the smallest population, has only three electors, Washington, DC has been assigned three electors. Each state has as many Electoral College votes as it has members in the House of Representatives, plus its two senators. This amendment does not include the right to vote in national elections for members of Congress or participate in the amendment process.

Background

In 1790 Secretary of the Treasury, Alexander Hamilton, proposed that the question of where the federal government should reside permanently should be solved by establishing a district under the jurisdiction of the federal government. The government at that time was functioning out of Philadelphia. President Washington was asked to choose a site. He picked an area on both sides of the Potomac River. Maryland and Virginia agreed to give up their parts of this designated area and the French engineer, Pierre Charles L'Enfant, was commissioned to design what became known as Washington DC, the District of Columbia. The government was moved to the new capital in 1800. George Washington was the only president who never functioned there.

Under Congress

At first Congress appointed all city officials, but gradually Washington was given a measure of home rule. Today the mayor, city council and school board are elected by the inhabitants who also have some control over local taxes. Congress still has the final say in all government matters. On the national level, Washington can now vote for the President of the United States, as defined in the **23rd Amendment**. As of 1970 the District of Columbia can send a delegate to the U.S. House of Representatives with the authority to vote in House committees, but not on the House floor where all members cast votes.

Layout

The city of Washington, situated on the Maryland side of the Potomac River, includes what is called Capitol Hill - the U.S. Capitol, congressional buildings, the Supreme Court Building, Library of Congress, the U.S. Botanical Garden and a private institution, the Folger Shakespeare Library. The city covers almost 70 square miles and has a current population of about 607,000 people. The land on the Virginia side of the Potomac, which was restored to Virginia in 1846, contains Arlington National Cemetery (under the authority of the Department of the Army) and the Washington National Airport.

Petition for Statehood

Nothing in the Constitution prohibits a district from becoming a state. In a 1980 local election the inhabitants of Washington, DC voted to apply for statehood following the legal steps laid down by Congress for territories:

1. A petition was sent to Congress requesting admission into the Union for the District of Columbia, September, 1983.
2. Congress' resolution authorizing the district to create a constitution was sent to and approved by the president.
3. A state constitution and state name, New Columbia, were submitted to Congress along with the assurance that an area would be preserved according to the U.S. Constitution **(Article 1, Sec. 8, Par. (17))** for the United States seat of government.
4. If and when a majority of both houses of Congress and then the president approved, and DC accepted any changes that might be indicated, statehood would be granted.

NOTE: It is true that once a territory or district is a sovereign state it can make any alterations, unless they are unconstitutional, that the inhabitants of the state request. However, there is no precedent for a state changing it's name without the approval of the federal government. In the case of Utah, that as a territory had been called Deseret (meaning "honeybee" in the Book of Mormon), the petition for statehood included the request that the existing name be retained. Congress changed the name to Utah after the Ute Indians who inhabited the region.

The Final Decision

DC's request for statehood was officially turned down in the House of Representatives, where petitions are first reviewed, in November of 1993. Most Republicans failed to vote for its passage. The district is primarily Democratic and, as a state, would probably add another Democrat in the House and two in the Senate. There are people, however, in and out of Washington who do not want to see our national capital involved in the politics of any party. Giving the district the right to vote for our presidents, who hopefully are primarily concerned with the affairs and needs of the nation as a whole, is as far as many Americans want to go at this time.

A Look at U.S. Island Government

CONSTITUTIONAL REFERENCE

Article IV, Sec. 3, Par.(2) - U.S. Territories and Other Property:

> The Congress shall have Power to dispose of and make all needful Rules and Regulations respecting the Territory or other Property belonging to the United States;

The Constitution has nothing to say about how U.S. territories should function other than to specify that they be under the control of Congress. Since they have different backgrounds and purposes, administration has been flexible and varied. Although our influence has waned in the Philippines and Panama Canal Zone, and two of our territories, Hawaii and Alaska, have become states, the United States still has responsibilities concerning different islands in the Atlantic and Pacific areas of the globe. The Commonwealth of Puerto Rico has already come close to petitioning for statehood.

Besides the District of Columbia, the islands of Guam, Puerto Rico, American Samoa and the Virgin Islands have a delegate in the U.S. Congress who can voice their islands' opinions and vote in congressional committees. No delegates vote on the House floor.

Islanders having American citizenship who decide to live in the United States pay taxes. They can vote at the state and federal level and in general have all of the privileges and responsibilities of other American citizens residing in this country.

The Island of Guam

Guam, the southern most island in the Mariana Pacific chain, that lies north of Australia, was acquired from Spain in 1898. Residents of Guam have U.S. citizenship, local self-government and a delegate in Congress. Andersen Air Force Base and Agana Naval Air Station are on Guam. Originally under the Navy, it is now in the hands of the Department of the Interior.

Midway Islands

These islands, discovered and annexed by the United States, lie close to Hawaii. They demonstrated their strategic value in WWII after the attack on Pearl Harbor. The Battle of Midway, our first decisive victory over the Japanese, was the turning point for the U.S. in the Pacific. Midway is under the supervision of the Department of the Navy.

The Palau Islands

The Palau Islands, near the Philippines, were taken from Japan in WWII and held in trust in a U.S. agreement with the United Nations under the Department of the Interior. In 1994 Palau voters adopted a Compact of Free Association with the United States in an effort to terminate their Trust Territory status. They became an independent republic by October of that year. The Palau Islands were the last of our UN Trust Territories.

Puerto Rico

Commonwealth Status

Columbus really did stop here on his second voyage in 1493. This Caribbean island, closer to Cuba than the United States, was ceded to the U.S. by Spain at the end of the Spanish-American War.

Puerto Ricans are self-governing American citizens with many American privileges. They do not pay U.S. taxes or vote for members of Congress or the president unless they take up residence in the U.S. Their delegate to Congress is known as a resident commissioner. Their constitution was approved by the U.S. Congress.

Background

The original settlers, the Arawak Indians, later blended with Spanish invaders. The official language is Spanish, but all school children are taught English. Americans and American industries have been on this island for many years. The 1990 Census placed their population at 3,522,037.

Election of '93

In early November of 1993, just before the District of Columbia was turned down for statehood, Puerto Rico had a local election to determine whether the island would become independent, remain in a commonwealth relationship with the United States, or petition for statehood. The returns indicated 48% wanted to remain a commonwealth and 46% favored statehood. Puerto Rico's governor predicted that in their next election they would opt for statehood.

SAMOA

The residents of this group of islands in the South Pacific are primarily of Polynesian descent. Until 1951 the U.S. had a naval base on the island of Tutuila, the only good harbor. Tutuila is in Eastern Samoa, which is a U.S. possession, and has a delegate in Congress. Western Samoa became an independent nation in 1962. Eastern Samoans are U.S. nationals, not citizens, and are under the Department of the Interior. Tuna fishing and processing are big industries here.

THE VIRGIN ISLANDS

The Virgin Islands lie east of Puerto Rico between the Caribbean Sea and Atlantic Ocean. St. Croix, St. John and St. Thomas Islands, with their numerous inlets, make up the American Virgin Islands. This was Danish territory sold to the United States for $25 million in 1917. England has control of six of the main islands. The U.S. islanders are self-governing

American citizens and have a delegate in Congress. They are under the Department of the Interior. St. Croix has the largest petroleum refinery in the world.

WAKE ISLAND

Wake is a Mid-Pacific island territory supervised by the Department of Interior when not under the jurisdiction of the military. It is primarily an Air Force and Navy refueling depot and a center for weather and oceanic research. Over time Wake's personnel (there are no natives) include the U.S. Air Force, U.S. civilians and contractors from Thailand.

Odds and Ends

Can the Government Take Your Property?

5th Amendment, last sentence (1791)

No person shall --- be deprived of life, liberty or property, without due process of law; nor shall private property be taken for public use, without just compensation.

14th Amendment, Sec. 1 (1868)

No State shall --- deprive any person of life, liberty, or property, without due process of law;

The 5th Amendment puts restrictions on the *federal* government taking private property. The 14th Amendment has extended "due process" to *state* governments concerning private property.

Key Phrases

due process
a fair execution of the law in U.S. courts insuring that no person's rights are denied.

eminent domain
the inherent right of the U.S. government to take private property for public use- a right claimed by all nations.

Our Growth and Development

Before leaving the Founding Fathers, it is important to understand the ever-growing size and complexity of the United States so that we can appreciate how far-sighted the creators of the Constitution were. It has met and survived every challenge the country has had to face because it was created to grow with us. Ours is an interaction. We mold and sustain the Constitution and it, in turn, molds and sustains us. It only functions in any period as well as the amount of caring and nurturing we the people are willing to give it. Our greatest difficulty is the fact that our understanding of the desires, needs and cultural differences of fellow Americans has a hard time keeping pace with the growth and development of the nation as a whole.

The United States moved at a fast clip until the 48 states on the mainland were in place. Then we waited 47 years before adding Alaska and Hawaii. Territory was acquired by annexation, exploration, staking of claims (particularly in the gold rush periods), making deals with tribes and countries, purchases and wars. People kept on coming into this country and people kept on moving West, stopped only by the Pacific Ocean. Those who lived in the Orient and islands of the Pacific were for the most part later arrivals. However, it is true that the city of San Francisco for a very long time has been a haven for many Asians.

Some states joined the Union in one piece, such as Hawaii and Alaska, while others were put together like jigsaw puzzles. As new territory developed Congress rearranged existing territories. Minnesota was part of seven different territories before the Territory of Minnesota was created in 1849.

Alaska, at the time of purchase, was considered to be our greatest folly. The Louisiana Purchase stands out as our all-time greatest achievement. Listed here are some of the ways in which we have enlarged our sphere.

Gains of the American Revolution, 1783

In addition to gaining the 13 colonies from Great Britain, we acquired territory that became the states of Ohio, Indiana, Illinois, Michigan and parts of Wisconsin, Minnesota, Mississippi and Alabama.

The Louisiana Purchase, 1803

The U.S. paid Napoleon Bonaparte of France approximately $15 million for land that included all or parts of the states of Montana, North and South Dakota, Colorado, Wyoming, Arkansas, Nebraska, Oklahoma, Iowa, Kansas, Louisiana, Missouri and Minnesota.

The Red River Cession, 1818

This treaty with Great Britain enlarged the boundaries of North and South Dakota and Minnesota.

Annexations of 1810-13 and Florida Cession, 1819

Spain extended the southern borders of Louisiana, Mississippi and Alabama, and ceded Florida to the U.S.

The Texas Annexation, 1845

With the annexation of the Republic of Texas came territory that ultimately formed parts of New Mexico, Wyoming, Colorado, Oklahoma and

Kansas. (Texas has functioned under six flags - Spain, France, Mexico, the Republic of Texas, the United States and the Confederacy.)

The Oregon Cession, 1846

This treaty with Great Britain gained the U.S. the areas of Washington, Oregon, Idaho and parts of Wyoming and Montana.

The Mexican Cession, 1848

At the end of our conflict with Mexico, in the Treaty of Guadalupe Hidalgo, the U.S. gave Mexico $15 million for land that formed all or parts of California, Arizona, Nevada, New Mexico, Wyoming, Colorado and Utah.

The Gadsen Purchase, 1853

This time the U.S. paid Mexico $10 million for the lower parts of Arizona and New Mexico. This exchange was so unpopular in Mexico that their leader, General Santa Anna, of the Alamo fame, was forced to leave the country. (Three cheers from Texas.)

The Alaskan Purchase, 1867

We paid Russia $7,200,000 - about two cents an acre - for what at the time was called "Seward's Folly," William H. Seward being our Secretary of State who negotiated the purchase. Today it should be called "Seward's Grand Surprise." (Three more cheers, Alaska!)

Chart of Our Growth and Development

Date of Statehood	State Name	State Background
1790 - May 29	13 Original States	All states ratified the Constitution by 1790
1791 - March 4	14 Vermont (VT)	Republic of Vermont 1777 - 1791
1792 - June 1	15 Kentucky (KY)	County in Virginia 1776 - 1792
1796 - June 1	16 Tennessee (TN)	Part of NC until 1789 U.S. territory 1789-1796
1803 - March 1	17 Ohio (OH)	U.S. territorial gain 1783 end of American Revolution
1812 - April 30	18 Louisiana (LA)	Louisiana Purchase 1803 Florida Cession 1819
1816 - December 11	19 Indiana (IN)	U.S. territorial gain 1783 end of American Revolution
1817 - December 10	20 Mississippi (MS)	U.S. territorial gain 1783 Florida Cession 1819
1818 - December 3	21 Illinois (IL)	U.S. territorial gain 1783 end of American Revolution
1819 - December 14	22 Alabama (AL)	U.S. territorial gain 1783 Florida Cession 1819
1820 - March 15	23 Maine (ME)	Part of Massachusetts 1677 - 1819
1821 - August 10	24 Missouri (MO)	Louisiana Purchase 1803
1836 - June 15	25 Arkansas (AR)	Louisiana Purchase 1803
1837 - January 26	26 Michigan (MI)	U.S. territorial gain 1783 end of American Revolution
1845 - March 3	27 Florida (FL)	Florida Cession 1819
1845 - December 29	28 Texas (TX)	Republic of Texas 1836 - 1845
1846 - December 28	29 Iowa (IA)	Louisiana Purchase 1803
1848 - May 29	30 Wisconsin (WI)	U.S. territorial gain 1783 end of American Revolution
1850 - September 9	31 California (CA)	Mexican Cession 1848
1858 - May 11	32 Minnesota (MN)	U.S. territorial gain 1783 Louisiana Purchase 1803 Red River Cession 1818
1859 - February 14	33 Oregon (OR)	Oregon Cession 1846
1861 - January 29	34 Kansas (KS)	Louisiana Purchase 1803 Texas Annexation 1845

Table (Continued)

Date of Statehood	State Name	State Background
1863 - June 20	35 West Virginia (WV)	Separated from Virginia 1863
1864 - October 31	36 Nevada (NV)	Mexican Cession 1848
1867 - March 1	37 Nebraska (NE)	Louisiana Purchase 1803
1876 - August 1	38 Colorado (CO)	Louisiana Purchase 1803 Texas Annexation 1845 Mexican Cession 1848
1889 - November 2	39 North Dakota (ND)	Louisiana Purchase 1803 Red River Cession 1818
1889 - November 2	40 South Dakota (SD)	ND and SD joint territory until statehood
1889 - November 8	41 Montana (MT)	Louisiana Purchase 1803 Oregon Cession 1846
1889 - November 11	42 Washington (WA)	Oregon Cession 1846
1890 - July 3	43 Idaho (ID)	Oregon Cession 1846
1890 - July 10	44 Wyoming (WY)	Louisiana Purchase 1803 Texas Annexation 1845 Oregon Cession 1846 Mexican Cession 1848
1896 - January 4	45 Utah (UT)	Mexican Cession 1848
1907 - November 16	46 Oklahoma (OK)	Louisiana Purchase 1803 Texas Annexation1845
1912 - January 6	47 New Mexico (NM)	Texas Annexation 1845 Mexican Cession 1848 Gadsen Purchase 1853
1912 - February 14	48 Arizona (AZ)	Mexican Cession 1848 Gadsen Purchase 1853
1959 - January 3	49 Alaska (AK)	Russian Purchase 1867
1959 - August 21	50 Hawaii (HI)	Kingdom of HI 1795-1893 Republic of HI 1893-1900 U.S. Territory 1900-1959

Part II

Balance of Power

Overview

Constitutional Reference

Article IV, Sec. 4 - The U.S. a Republic:

The United States shall guarantee to every State in this Union a Republican Form of Government...

Defining a Republic

A republic is defined as a government in which the control resides with the people or a certain portion of the people, with law making and administrative powers given to officers who are elected by and represent the people. But can there be a guarantee? Our Founding Fathers believed this republic would survive as long as the people were vigilant about keeping it alive. The Roman Republic, a strong light in the dark halls of ancient history, did ultimately self-destruct. It is of value to understand why.

Political Structure of the Roman Republic

Roman nobles dissolved their monarchy and established a republic in 509 B.C. which lasted until 27 B.C. - almost 500 years. They carried over two things from their era of kings: the Senate, a group composed of heads of the prominent families who had been advisors to the king, and the citizens assemblies that had been allowed to vote on decisions made by the king and Senate. To these the republic added two elected consuls to run the government. Consuls were only elected for one year and could veto each other's decisions. Senators were in office for life. The Senate was obviously the most important body. It conducted foreign affairs, was in charge of government finances and passed all official orders.

The Laws of the Twelve Tablets

The Roman code of law, which was published about 450 B.C., put into writing what were already the accepted legal practices. It ultimately formed the basis of legal systems in most of Western Europe and our own hemisphere. Conquered territories were allowed to keep their own laws, customs and religions so long as they were not in conflict with Roman law. Roman citizenship meant protection and privileges under Roman law and was ultimately granted to most of the conquered people.

High Point of the Roman Republic

Rome reached its peak during the 200's and 100's B.C. In that period Roman citizens took great pride in their government and army (the army did not just fight, it also built roads, bridges and other things needed for public use). In that period Rome controlled the entire area of the Mediterranean Sea, making deep inroads into North Africa, Europe and the Middle East. It was considered to have the world's most balanced government.

Fall of the Roman Republic

The Roman Republic collapsed after 20 years of civil war among leading factions, which allowed a strong individual, Octavian (called Augustus), to step into the breach and become Rome's first emperor. The Roman Empire continued for some time, but the power of the Senate and the people declined. Ultimately emperors became so removed from the people that they began to be worshipped as gods after death.

Constitutional Reference

Article VI, Par. (2) - Constitutional Supremacy:

This Constitution, and the Laws of the United States which shall be made in Pursuance thereof; and all Treaties made, or which shall be made, under the Authority of the United States, shall be the supreme Law of the Land; and the Judges in every State shall be bound thereby, any Thing in the Constitution or Laws of any State to the Contrary notwithstanding.

Article VI, Par. (2) puts the legal authority of the United States Constitution above and beyond that of the states, but one of the most outstanding characteristics of our Constitution is its balance of power. We are a republic and have a *federal* government, which means that power is not centralized. In this country the power is divided between the central government (which is further divided) and the states. Since we call our central government in Washington the federal government, that is the way it will be addressed in this book.

Constitutional Reference

Summary of Article IV, Sec. 4, - Federal Support for the States:

The United States guarantees protection for each state against invasion; "and on Application of the Legislature, or of the Executive (when the Legislature cannot be convened) against domestic Violence."

There are many things the federal government will do when a state formally requests aid through its state legislature or executive (governor), such as in the case of domestic violence or natural disasters. This is procedure for internal problems. When it comes to external problems, such as invasion, the federal government needs no prompting to deliver help. This spread of power can make our progress more cumbersome than in other types of governments. However, it is clearly defined in the United States Constitution that we will get support from our central government as needed, and is a safeguard against dictatorial takeovers by that governing body.

Balance of Power in the Federal Government

Constitutional References

The Legislative Branch that Makes the Laws:
Article I, Sec. 1.

All legislative Powers herein granted shall be vested in a Congress of the United States, which shall consist of a Senate and House of Representatives.

The Executive Branch that Carries Out the Laws:
Article II, Sec. 1, Par.(1).

The executive Power shall be vested in a President of the United States of America.

The Judicial Branch that Interprets the Laws:
Article III, Sec. 1.

The judicial Power of the United States, shall be vested in one supreme Court, and in such inferior Courts as the Congress may from time to time ordain and establish.

Qualifications, Term Limits and Representation

Constitutional References

Article I, Sec. 2, Par. (1) and (2) - House of Representatives
17th Amendment, Par. (1) and
Article I, Sec. 3, Par. (3) - The Senate
Article II, Sec. 1, Par. (1) and (5) - The President
Article III, Sec. 1 - The Supreme Court

Qualifications

	Age	Citizenship	Residency
House of Representatives	25	7 years	state where elected
Senate	30	9 years	state where elected
President	35	natural born citizen	U.S. resident 14 yrs.
Supreme Court	---	------	United States

Length of Term and Representation

	Term	Representation
House of Representatives	2 years	state where elected
Senate	6 years	state where elected
President	4 years	The United States
Supreme Court	life appointment	U.S. Constitution

NOTE: Qualifications are the same for the Vice President as they are for the President (**12th Amendment**, last sentence).

Odds and Ends

Who Says What in Washington?

Article I, Sec. 5, Par. (3) - Congressional Records:

Each House shall keep a Journal of its Proceedings, and from time to time publish the same, excepting such Parts as may in their Judgment require Secrecy; and the yeas and Nays of the Members of either House on any question shall, at the Desire of one Fifth of those Present, be entered on the Journal.

Article II, Sec. 2, Par. (1) - Presidential Records:

The President --- may require the Opinion, in writing, of the principal Officer in each of the executive Departments, upon any Subject relating to the Duties of their respective Offices, ...

All cases before the Supreme Court including the opinions of all justices are on file for future reference and public review.

Write: The United States Government Printing Office
Superintendent of Documents
Washington, DC 20402

Congress

The Legislative Branch that Makes the Laws

> The Congress shall have Power --- To make all Laws which shall be necessary and proper for carrying into Execution the foregoing Powers, and all other Powers vested by this Constitution in the Government of the United States, or in any Department or Officer thereof.
>
> **Article I, Sec. 8, Par. (18)**
> U.S. Constitution

It is not surprising that **Article I** concerns Congress and is the longest and most detailed article in the Constitution. Congress is our largest governing body, the closest to the American people, and responsible for the creation of our laws.

Some congressional powers have already been covered and others will be in the chapters to come. This chapter centers around congressional representation, financial powers, and the joint authority of Congress with the president in the areas of law making and control of the Armed Forces.

REPRESENTATION

Article I, Sec. 2, Par. (3) contains the original formula used by the states to determine their number of members in the House of Representatives. It was changed after the Civil War by the **14th Amendment, Sec. 2** to include former slaves, all of whom had become U.S. citizens.

What **Article I** established that still applies is the census taken every 10 years which is used to equate the number of representatives each state should have. The formula is not the same today, but the basic concept has been sustained.

Constitutional References

Article I, Sec. 2, Par. (3), last sentence

The First House of Representatives

> The Number of Representatives shall not exceed one for every thirty Thousand, but each State shall have at Least one Representative; and until such enumeration's (population counts) shall be made, the State of New Hampshire shall be entitled to choose three, Massachusetts eight, Rhode-Island and Providence Plantations one, Connecticut five, New-York six, New Jersey four, Pennsylvania eight, Delaware one, Maryland six, Virginia ten, North Carolina five, South Carolina five and Georgia three.

The Constitution says nothing about establishing state districts, but for a long time states have been divided into districts that reflect their census population figures and number of allotted members in the House of Representatives.

In most states residents vote for the House candidates who run for office in their district. In states that have only one member in the House, called representatives at large, the residents vote as they would for their senators. (See *The Way of Politics and Elections in America* - how and when the popular election of senators was introduced.)

In case you have ever wondered why some senators seem to be up for election every two years when they have terms that are supposed to last six years, here is your answer.

Article I, Sec. 3, Par. (2) - The Senate:

> Immediately after they shall be assembled in Consequence of the first Election, they (the Senators) shall be divided as equally as may be into three Classes. The Seats of the Senators of the first Class shall be vacated at the Expiration of the second Year, of the second Class at the Expiration of the fourth Year, and of the third Class at the Expiration of the sixth Year, so that one third may be chosen every second Year;

This process has created smoother vacancy transitions. After the first round all Senators have served six year terms with 1/3rd up for election every two years, which makes the Senate a continuous body. Members of the House of Representatives from the beginning have been up for election every two years. Only the number of House members for each state varies with population changes.

The First U.S. House of Representatives
Specified in Article I, Sec. 2, Par. (3)

New Hampshire	3	Pennsylvania	8
Massachusetts	8	Delaware	1
Connecticut	5	Maryland	6
New York	6	Virginia	10
New Jersey	4	North Carolina	5
Rhode Island & Providence Plantations	1	South Carolina	5
		Georgia	3

Composition of the First U.S. Congress in 1787

States	*Senate*	*House of Representatives*
13	26 members	65 members

Composition of the U.S. Congress in 1997

States	*Senate*	*House of Representatives*
50	100 members	435 members

The Population of the United States

1790 = 3,929,214 The 1990's = 248,709,873

STATE POPULATIONS AND REPRESENTATION HOUSE OF REPRESENTATIVES - 104TH CONGRESS

1990 Resident Census Populations

State	Population	House of Rep.	State	Population	House of Rep.
Alabama	4,040,587	7	Montana	799,065	1
Alaska	550,043	1	Nebraska	1,578,385	3
Arizona	3,665,228	6	Nevada	1,201,833	2
Arkansas	2,350,725	4	New Hampshire	1,109,252	2
California	29,760,021	52	New Jersey	7,730,188	13
Colorado	3,294,394	6	New Mexico	1,515,069	3
Connecticut	3,287,116	6	New York	17,990,455	31
Delaware	666,168	1	North Carolina	6,628,637	12
Florida	12,937,926	23	North Dakota	638,800	1
Georgia	6,478,216	11	Ohio	10,847,115	19
Hawaii	1,108,229	2	Oklahoma	3,145,585	6
Idaho	1,006,749	2	Oregon	2,842,321	5
Illinois	11,430,602	20	Pennsylvania	11,881,643	21
Indiana	5,544,159	10	Rhode Island	1,003,464	2

Iowa	2,776,755	5	South Carolina	3,486,703	6
Kansas	2,477,574	4	South Dakota	696,004	1
Kentucky	3,685,296	6	Tennessee	4,877,185	9
Louisiana	4,219,973	7	Texas	16,986,510	30
Maine	1,227,928	2	Utah	1,722,850	3
Maryland	4,781,468	8	Vermont	562,758	1
Massachusetts	6,016,425	10	Virginia	6,187,358	11
Michigan	9,295,297	16	Washington	4,866,692	9
Minnesota	4,375,099	8	West Virginia	1,793,477	3
Mississippi	2,573,216	5	Wisconsin	4,891,769	9
Missouri	5,117,073	9	Wyoming	453,588	1

STATE POLITICAL PARTY REPRESENTATION HOUSE (H) AND SENATE(S) - 104TH CONGRESS

Alabama*	(H) mix - (S) mix	Montana	(H) D- (S) mix
Alaska	(H) R- (S) R	Nebraska	(H) R- (S) D
Arizona	(H) mix - (S) R	Nevada	(H) R- (S) D
Arkansas	(H) mix - (S) D	New Hampshire	(H) R - (S) R
California	(H) mix - (S) D	New Jersey	(H) mix - (S) D
Colorado*	(H) mix - (S) R	New Mexico	(H) mix - (S) mix
Connecticut	(H) mix - (S) D	New York	(H) mix - (S) mix
Delaware	(H) R- (S) mix	North Carolina	(H) mix - (S) R
Florida	(H) mix - (S) mix	North Dakota	(H) D - (S) D
Georgia*	(H) mix - (S) mix	Ohio	(H) mix - (S) mix
Hawaii	(H) D- (S) D	Oklahoma	(H) mix - (S) R
Idaho	(H) R- (S) R	Oregon	(H) mix - (S) R
Illinois	(H) mix - (S) D	Pennsylvania	(H) mix - (S) R
Indiana	(H) mix - (S) R	Rhode Island	(H) D- (S) mix
Iowa	(H) R- (S) mix	South Carolina	(H) mix - (S) mix
Kansas	(H) R- (S) R	South Dakota	(H) D- (S) mix
Kentucky	(H) mix - (S) mix	Tennessee	(H) mix - (S) R
Louisiana	(H) mix - (S) D	Texas	(H) mix - (S) R
Maine	(H) mix - (S) R	Utah	(H) mix - (S) R
Maryland	(H) mix - (S) D	Vermont*	(H) Ind.- (S) mix

Massachusetts	(H) mix - (S) D	Virginia	(H) mix - (S) mix
Michigan	(H) mix - (S) mix	Washington	(H) mix - (S) mix
Minnesota	(H) mix - (S) mix	West Virginia	(H) D- (S) D
Mississippi	(H) mix - (S) R	Wisconsin	(H) mix - (S) D
Missouri	(H) mix - (S) R	Wyoming	(H) R- (S) R

*Party distribution changes January - April, 1995 include a shift of Democrats Sen. Richard Shelby (AL), Sen Ben Nighthorse Campbell (CO) and Representative Nathan Deal (GA) to the Republican party. Vermont's single House member is an Independent.

It is estimated that our census is about 1.4% inaccurate. Aliens are not screened out and missing persons are not accounted for. Before 1990 overseas military were not included. The census for the 1990s, which will be in effect until the year 2000, has added 923,000 overseas personnel by assigning them to the states they call home.

In response to a lawsuit on the part of several states concerning citizens not accounted for, the Supreme Court, in March of 1996, upheld the 1990 U.S. Census. The Court decided that the government had acted in good faith and this census should stand unaltered until the 21st century.

FINANCE

The Constitution leaves no doubt that Congress is in charge of the finances of the United States, but also establishes some limitations.

Constitutional References

Article I, Sec. 8, Par. (1) - Raising Revenue
Article I, Sec. 8, Par. (2) - Borrowing Money
Article I, Sec. 8, Par. (5) - Coining and Regulating Money
Article I, Sec. 8, Par. (6) - Counterfeiting

Congressional Financial Powers

1. Lay and collect taxes (levied on people, property or businesses); duties or imposts (taxes on exports or imports); and excises (indirect taxes on

such things as manufactured goods and licenses), to be used to pay any national debts and provide for the common defense and welfare of the United States.

2. Borrow money on the credit of the United States from the sale of government securities to banks, businesses or individuals.
3. Coin money and regulate its value and the value for foreign money. Fix the standards of weights and measures.
4. Provide for the punishment of counterfeiting United States money and securities, such as government bonds, treasury certificates and treasury notes.

THE CONSTITUTION CONCERNING NATIONAL DEBTS

Constitutional References

Article VI, Par. (1) (1787) - U.S. responsibility for the debts of the Articles of Confederation upheld:

All Debts contracted and Engagements entered into, before the Adoption of this Constitution, shall be as valid against the United States under this Constitution, as under the Confederation.

14th Amendment, Sec. 4, last part (1868) - U.S. responsibility for Confederate debts end of the Civil War denied:

But neither the United States nor any State shall assume or pay any debt or obligation incurred in aid of insurrection or rebellion against the United States, or any claim for the loss or emancipation of any slave; but all such debts, obligations and claims shall be held illegal and void.

NOTE: The Constitution never refers to the Civil War in a direct way. The subject is addressed only in general terms such as "rebellion" and "insurrection." The fact that these states withdraw from the Union to form their own government is never acknowledged.

In the area of compensation, all funds for salaries, including their own, are financed by Congress out of the national treasury. The Constitution does not specify amounts.

Constitutional References

Article I, Sec. 6, Par. (1) - Congress:

The Senators and Representatives shall receive a Compensation for their Services, to be ascertained by Law, and paid out of the Treasury of the United States.

Article II, Sec. 1, Par. (7) - The President:

The President shall, at stated Times, receive for his Services, a Compensation, which shall neither be encreased nor diminished during the Period for which he shall have been elected, and he shall not receive within that Period any other Emolument (fee or salary) from the United States, or any of them (the states).

Article III, Sec. 1, 2nd Sentence - The Supreme Court and Lower Federal Courts:

The Judges, both of the supreme and inferior Courts --- shall, at stated Times, receive for their Services, a Compensation, which shall not be diminished during their Continuance in Office.

Mindful of the attitude of the American people concerning government employee raises, Congress has provided for a review every four years of all salary categories for cabinet officers, federal judges and members of Congress by a special commission. This commission's findings are reviewed by the president. If everyone agrees, salary changes are implemented.

Constitutional References

Article I, Sec. 8, Par. (1), last part - Uniform Taxation
Article I, Sec. 9, Par. (7) - Treasury Procedures and Accountability

Congressional Financial Limitations

1. All duties, imposts and excises must be uniform throughout the United States.
2. No money shall be drawn from the U.S. treasury except through appropriations made by law; and a regular statement and account of the receipts and all expenditures of public money is to be published from time to time.

Making the Laws

Constitutional Reference

Article I, Sec. 7, Par. (1) through (3) - Passing a Bill:

1. All bills passed by the house of Representatives and Senate are sent to the president of the United States for approval.
2. If the president approves, he signs the bill and it becomes the law. If he doesn't approve, he vetoes the bill and returns it, along with his objections, to the house that has originated the bill. All bills related to revenue originate in the house of Representatives.
3. Any bill not returned by the president within 10 days (Sunday excepted) will automatically become law. If Congress is in recess before the 10 days are up, the bill dies unless it is signed by the president. This is known as a *pocket veto.*
4. When a bill is returned with a veto, the house that originated the bill must have a 2/3rd majority instead of a simple majority to pass the bill again, this time with the president's objections, to the other house for approval.
5. The other house must also have a 2/3rd majority in favor of the bill for it to become law.

This procedure applies to every resolution, order or vote involving both houses of Congress, except adjournment of the two houses. Every bill is given a number that indicates what Congress signed it and who the members were at the time it was signed.

The amendment process takes place between Congress and the states only. The president is not involved.

Final Thoughts

Congress was given such broad authority in the area of finance it was deemed advisable to give the president veto power in the law-making process.

In the case of territorial and district requests for statehood, if both houses of Congress and then the president favor a petition it is granted. (Washington DC did not get beyond the house of Representatives.) But when it comes to lawmaking, if Congress can muster enough votes, the presidential veto can be overridden. This is where politics plays such a strong role that was not foreseen at the time the Constitution was written.

Whose War Was Vietnam?

Constitutional References

Article I, Sec. 8, Par. (10) through (16) - Military Powers of Congress
Article II, Sec. 2, Par. (1) and (2) - Military Powers of the President
Article VI, Par. (2) - Treaties, the Supreme Law
2nd Amendment - Right of the States to Sustain Armed Militias

Summary of Military Powers of Congress

1. Define and punish serious crimes on the high seas.
2. Raise and support armies; no appropriation of money to be longer than two years.
3. Provide and maintain a navy.
4. Make rules for regulation of land and naval forces.
5. Organize, arm and govern state Militias as needed for the United States.
6. Suppress all insurrections and invasions.

7. Declare war; make rules concerning captures on land and water.

Summary of Military Powers of the President

1. Power to make treaties with advise and consent of 2/3rd of Senate present.
2. Grant reprieves and pardons, except concerning impeachment.
3. Commander in Chief of the Armed Forces. (In times of war, declared or undeclared, this title gives presidents unprecedented powers.)

The Armed Forces

Although the Constitution only specifically refers to the Army, Navy and Militia, military forces of all kinds come under Congress and the president as part of the Armed Forces - an implied constitutional power of Congress. (See *Supreme Court.*)

Air Force - made a separate department from the army in 1947.

Marine Corps - a separate branch within the Department of the Navy. Created in 1775 to help fight in the American Revolution. Considered to be the Navy's land force.

Coast Guard - the oldest sea going force in the nation. A branch of the Department of Transportation, but attached to the Navy in time of war. Enforces U.S. maritime laws.

Militia - originally a state citizen protection group, now includes the Army National Guard, Army Reserve, Marine Corps and Naval Reserve, Air Force Reserve and Air National Guard.

NOTE: THE CONSTITUTION AUTHORIZES CONGRESS TO CALL IN STATE MILITIAS TO DEFEND THE LAWS OF THE LAND AND HELP SUPPRESS INSURRECTIONS OR INVASIONS, BUT RESERVES TO THE STATES THE APPOINTMENT OF OFFICERS. TRAINING IS CARRIED OUT BY THE STATES ACCORDING TO THE DISCIPLINE PRESCRIBED BY CONGRESS WHEN MILITIAS ARE UNDER THE JURISDICTION OF THE UNITED STATES.

VIETNAM

Background

Vietnam, Laos and Cambodia made up the French colony of Indochina from the 1800's to the 1940's. During WWII the region was under Japanese control. The conflict between France and the North Vietnamese Communists under Ho Chi Minh began in 1946 after WWII and terminated when a cease fire was achieved in 1954. Two governments were established. The Ho Chi Minh Communist government, North of the 17th Parallel, was backed by China and the U.S.S.R. The anti-Communist government south of the 17th Parallel, with headquarters in Saigon, was reinforced with U.S. military supplies and technical aid. A similar arrangement had been made in Korea and was still holding. France completely withdrew from Indochina.

U.S. Presidential War Years

1956 - 1959 North Vietnam was gaining control of areas through terrorist attacks on South Vietnam. President Dwight Eisenhower (R) increased U.S. military presence in South Vietnam. President John F. Kennedy (D) followed the Eisenhower policy.

1965 - 1969 The situation was worsening. By 1965 President Lyndon Johnson (D) supported increased bombing of North Vietnam and more U.S. ground involvement. Our troop buildup in South Vietnam accelerated from 60,000 in 1965 to over 543,000 by 1969.

January 1973 President Richard Nixon (R) finally achieved a cease fire that pushed the North Vietnamese back to the 17th Parallel. The U.S. made a rapid evacuation of Vietnam.

1975 With the U.S. out of the way, North Vietnam again pushed South, joining forces with Communists in Laos and Cambodia. By 1975 Indochina was virtually a Communist dominated region. This outcome was exactly what France and then the United States had tried to prevent.

Looking Back

1. The Vietnam War was one of the longest, most futile and unpopular wars in the history of our country.
2. U.S. patriotism was at an all-time low. Some military personnel involved developed long lasting emotional problems, a condition identified as Post-Traumatic Stress Disorder.
3. We were never able to get the cooperation of North Vietnam in the period in which it was vital to have it in order to recover our prisoners of war.
4. It is now estimated that at least 55,000 Americans died and another 365,000 were wounded in this war. The monetary cost to the U.S. was in excess of $150 billion. U.S. bombing of Vietnam was four times greater than the combined British and U.S. bombing of all of Germany in WWII. The total death toll in Vietnam was in the millions with over ten million South Vietnamese fleeing from the country when the U.S. withdrew.
5. A chemical, Agent Orange, used by the U.S. to clear the jungle of Vietnam, may have permanently damaged the land and was deadly for some of the human beings exposed to it. Cases have been going before courts in the country concerning this chemical's lethal effects on U.S. soldiers.
6. In this conflict there was no declared war or official peace treaty. Congress appropriated the money, but both Congress and the American people reached the point of feeling that we were being swept along by a war that would have no end and was not of our choosing.

The Situation Today

1. Vietnam is finally began to release data and remains of our military personnel listed as missing in action. As of 1994 about 2,250 were still not accounted for.
2. Amnesty (a general pardon) has been granted to all Americans who left the country and established residence in other parts of the world, primarily Canada, solely to avoid the draft.

3. The War Powers Act passed by Congress in 1973 made presidents more accountable to Congress in this area of foreign affairs. They now seek more global support before committing the U.S. in world conflicts, as President Bush successfully demonstrated in the Gulf War. (Presidents Bush in Panama and Clinton in Haiti called these interventions "police actions.")
4. The Vietnam War Memorial in Washington DC has given America a belated but sincere opportunity to thank those who suffered and died in this war because America asked them to become involved in it.
5. On July 12, 1995 President Clinton announced that the United States was officially opening diplomatic relations with Vietnam. This move met with the approval of Vietnam veteran, Vice President Al Gore, and veterans in Congress.

Disabled American Public Awareness Program (1994)

"Disabled veterans need to know what's available to them free of charge from the DAV --- If any friends or relatives are disabled veterans please help this outreach effort --- Information on all DAV services is available from:

Disabled American Veterans National Headquarters
P.O. Box 14301
Cincinnati, OH 45250-0301

How to Reach Congress

The proceedings of Congress are also available to the public. Congressional journals cover acts, resolutions and votes; the Congressional Record reports what is actually said in each house.

Odds and Ends

When is the Vice President a Part of Congress?

Article I, Sec. 2, Par. (5) - Speaker of the House:

The House of Representatives shall choose
their speaker and other Officers;

Article I, Sec. 3, Par. (4) - President of the Senate:

The Vice President of the United States shall be President of the Senate, but shall have no Vote unless they be equally divided.

Article I, Sec. 3, Par. (5) - President Pro Tempore of the Senate:

The Senate shall chuse their other Officers and also a President pro tempore, in the Absence of the Vice President, or when he shall exercise the Office of President of the United States.

NOTE: The president pro tempore is selected by the Senate majority party and can vote on any matter before the Senate.

Key Legal Phrase:

pro tempore

(Latin) the time being; temporary

The President

The Executive Branch that Carries Out the Laws

I do solemnly swear (or affirm) that I will faithfully execute the Office of President of the United States, and will to the best of my Ability, preserve, protect and defend the Constitution of the United States.

Presidential Oath of Office
Article II, Sec. 1, Par. (8)
U.S. Constitution

PRESIDENTS OF THE UNITED STATES

GEORGE WASHINGTON through BILL CLINTON

Coding:

F = Federalists
D/R = Democratic Republicans
D = Democrats
W = Whigs
UR = Union Republicans
R = Republicans
VP = Vice President

Ratings:

Historian performance ratings of the first 34 presidents (Wyatt Blassingame, The Look-it-Up Book of Presidents, 1993). Historians wait to see what lasting impact a president's performance has on the nation before giving a rating.

Name	Lifespan	Party	Rating	Term as President
1. George Washington	Birth-VA 1732-1799	---	great	1789-1797 Established 2-terms presidency
2. John Adams	Birth-MA 1735-1826	F	near great	1797-1801 1 term
3. Thomas Jefferson	Birth-VA 1743-1826	D/R	great to near great	1801-1809 2 terms
4. James Madison	Birth-VA 1751-1836	D/R	average	1809-1917 2 terms
5. James Monroe	Birth-VA 1758-1831	D/R	average	1817-1825 2 terms
6. John Quincy Adams	Birth-MA 1767-1848	D/R	average	1825-1829 1 term
7. Andrew Jackson	Birth-SC 1767-1845	D	great to near great	1829-1837 2 terms
8. Martin van Buren	Birth-NY 1782-1862	D	average	1837-1841 1 term
9. WM. Henry Harrison	Birth-VA 1773-1841	W	---	In 1841 Died of pneumonia after one month in office
10. John Tyler	Birth-VA 1790-1862	W	below average	1841-1845 VP who finished Harrison's term
11. James Knox Polk	Birth-NC 1795-1849	D	near great	1845-1849 Finished 1 term too ill to continued
12. Zachary Taylor	Birth-VA 1784-1850	W	below average	1849-1850 Suddenly ill, died July 9, 1850
13. Millard Fillmore	Birth-NY 1800-1874	W	below average	1850-1853 VP who finished Taylor's term
14. Franklin Pierce	Birth-NH 1804-1869	D	below average	1853-1857 1 term
15. James Buchanan	Birth-PA 1791-1868	D	below average	1857-1861 1 term

Table (Continued)

Name	Lifespan	Party	Rating	Term as President
16. Abraham Lincoln	Birth-KY 1809-1865	UR	great	1861-1865 Assassinated April 14, 1865
17. Andrew Johnson	Birth-NC 1808-1875	UR	near great to below average	1865-1869 VP who finished Lincoln's 2nd term
18. Ulysses S. Grant	Birth-OH 1822-1885	R	failure	1869-1877 2 terms
19. Rutherford B. Hayes	Birth-OH 1822-1893	R	average	1877-1881 1 term
20. James A. Garfield	Birth-OH 1831-1881	R	---	1881 Assassinated July 2, 1881
21 Chester A. Arthur	Birth-VT 1829-1886	R	average	1881-1885 VP who finished Garfield's term
22. Grover Cleveland	Birth-NJ 1837-1908	D	near great	1885-1889 1st term
23. Benjamin Harrison	Birth-OH 1833-1901	R	average	1889-1893 1 term
24. Grover Cleveland	Birth-NJ 1837-1908	D	near great	1893-1897 2nd term
25. William Mckinley	Birth-OH 1843-1901	R	average	1897-1901 Assassinated Sept. 6, 1901
26. Theodore Roosevelt	Birth-NY 1858-1919	R	near great	1901-1909 VP who finished Mckinley's 2nd term & one of his own
27. WM. Howard Taft	Birth-OH 1857-1930	R	average	1909-1913 1 term
28. Woodrow Wilson	Birth-VA 1856-1924	D	great	1913-1921 2 terms, ill of stroke all last year in office
29. Warren G. Harding	Birth-OH 1865-1923	R	failure	1921-1923 Suddenly ill and died August 2, 1923

Table (Continued)

30. Calvin Coolidge	Birth-VT 1872-1933	R	below average	1923-1929 VP who finished Harding's term and one of his own.
31. Herbert C. Hoover	Birth-IA 1874-1964	R	average	1929-1933 1 term
32. Franklin D. Roosevelt	Birth-NY 1882-1945	D	great	1933-1945 Died of a stroke April 12, 1945
33. Harry S Truman	Birth-MO 1884-1972	D	near great	1945-1953 VP who finished Roosevelt's 4th term and one of his own
34. Dwight D. Eisenhower	Birth-TX 1890-1969	R	average	1953-1961 2 terms
35. John F. Kennedy	Birth-MA 1917-1963	D	---	1961-1963 Assassinated Nov. 22, 1963
36. Lyndon B. Johnson	Birth-TX 1908-1973	D	---	1963-1969 VP who finished Kennedy's term and one of his own
37. Richard M. Nixon	Birth-CA 1913-1994	R	---	1969-1974 Resigned August 14, 1974
38. Gerald R. Ford	Birth-NE 1913-	R	---	1974-1977 Finished Nixon's 2nd term
39. James E. Carter	Birth-GA 1924-	D	---	1977-1981 1 term
40. Ronald W. Reagan	Birth-IL 1911-	R	---	1981-1989 2 terms
41. George H.W. Bush	Birth-MA 1924	R	---	1981-1989 2 terms
42. William J. Clinton	Birth-AR 1946-	D	---	1993-

VACANCIES

The President of the United States is our government official the most directly connected to all of the people. Possibly for that reason he has become our national symbol and, at times, a target. Four presidents have been assassinated while in office.

Abraham Lincoln

The first presidential assassination, that of Abraham Lincoln, was accomplished by the actor John Wilkes Booth. His exact reason has never been clarified, but it did take place just five days after Lee's surrender of all Confederate troops to Grant.

James A. Garfield

President Garfield was shot by Charles Giteau, a disgruntled man the President had denied a government job.

William McKinley

President McKinley was shot by anarchist, Leon Czolgosz, who didn't believe in government.

John F. Kennedy

Real cause of this assassination has not been determined because the alleged killer, Lee Harvey Oswald, was in turn shot and killed before he got to trial by an enraged Dallas citizen named Jack Ruby. The investigating committee, under the direction of Supreme Court Chief Justice Earl Warren, left a number of questions unresolved.

Four other presidents died of natural causes and one has resigned. President Polk did finish his first term, but was too ill to run for a second and died soon after leaving office. Woodrow Wilson was so incapacitated in the last year of his second term that his communication with the outside world was primarily handled by his wife.

In the history of our country a number of vice presidents and members of Congress also for various reasons have left office before their terms expired. The Constitution has addressed the problem of vacancies in several articles and amendments.

Constitutional References

Congressional Vacancies

17th Amendment, Par. (2) (1913)-
modifies Article I, Sec. 2, Par. (4)
Article II, Sec. 2, Par. (3)

Presidential Vacancies

Article II, Sec. 1, Par. (6)
20th Amendment, Sec. 3 and 4 (1933)
(Congress has never acted on Sec. 4)
25th Amendment (1967)

The **20th Amendment** extends **Article II, Sec. 1, Par. (6)**. It covers the president elect and vice president elect, describing what course should be taken if the president elect is unable to fill the office.

The **25th Amendment** further extends **Article II, Sec. 1, Par. (6)** and covers procedures concerning the inability of a president to "discharge the powers and duties of his office".

In A Nutshell

1. If Congress is in session, congressional vacancies are filled by the state affected until the next election.
2. If the Senate is in recess, the president can fill vacancies of any kind that occur which will expire at the end of their next session.
3. If the president is temporarily out of office, the vice president is Acting President.
4. If the president is permanently out of office, the vice president becomes President of the United States.

5. If the vice president is permanently out of office, the president, with approval of the majority vote of both houses of Congress, appoints a new vice president.
6. Conflict concerning succession it is resolved by Congress.

PRESIDENTIAL SUCCESSION

Next in line after the President and Vice President:

1. Speaker of the House
2. President pro tempcre of the Senate

Following these congressional leaders are the heads of departments in the order in which their departments were created.

A department head would only serve until a speaker of the House or president pro tempore of the Senate met the qualifications in the Constitution for the office of president - be at least 35 years old, a natural born citizen and a resident within the United States for a minimum of 14 years.

The first four departments - State, Treasury, War and Justice - were created by George Washington. As the nation grew, so did the need for more departments. These are the heads of departments in existence in the Clinton presidency.

1. Secretary of State
2. Secretary of the Treasury
3. Secretary of Defense (originally known as the Secretary of War)
4. Attorney General of the Justice Department
5. Secretary of the Interior
6. Secretary of Agriculture
7. Secretary of Commerce
8. Secretary of Labor
9. Secretary of Health and Human Resources
10. Secretary of Housing and Urban Development

11. Secretary of Transportation

12. Secretary of Energy

13. Secretary of Education

14. Secretary of Veterans Affairs

(Departments of the Army, Navy and Air Force are not included)

None of these people has been called upon to replace a president, but the possibility came close in the Nixon Administration. However, even then the Executive Branch was not mortally wounded and the country was able to go on about its business.

PRESIDENTIAL AND VICE PRESIDENTIAL

Successions of the Nixon Administration

Background

This president had been in politics all of his adult life - in the House of Representatives, the Senate, and for eight years Dwight Eisenhower's vice president. He became the first American president to visit and begin a relationship with Communist China; created the first arms control treaty with the Soviet Union; and brought an end to U.S. involvement in Vietnam. He will always be remembered for his contributions in the area of foreign affairs. A petty second election campaign incident ultimately cost him and his top aids the second term in office.

Watergate

In the campaign of '72, some Republican election committee people sponsored a break-in of the Washington DC Watergate building complex with the intent to photograph documents and plant electronic bugs in the Democratic campaign headquarters offices. The intruders were caught. President Nixon denied knowing anything about the incident.

The Vice President

Then Spiro T. Agnew was accused of taking illegal payments for services rendered before and after he was in the office of the vice president. These charges were never acted on officially. However, Agnew later pleaded "no contest" to the accusation that he had cheated on his income tax and resigned from office in October, 1973.

President Nixon appointed, with the approval of Congress, House Representative Gerald Ford to replace Spiro Agnew.

The Watergate Showdown

Nixon moved into his second term trying for business as usual, but the Watergate incident would not go away. Finally the Supreme Court ordered Nixon to turn over some tapes concerning his conversations with staff members. The tapes indicated that, although he had not known about the original incident, he had been party to its cover up.

The House of Representatives was gathering information for an impeachment the Senate appeared to be ready to support. Nixon made the decision to resign.

On August 14, 1974, Gerald Ford, the man who had been appointed to both the office of vice president and president, replaced Richard Nixon, the only president to ever resign from office.

President Ford appointed Nelson Rockefeller as his vice president and pardoned Richard Nixon. All of the other persons involved in the various scandals of this administration faced civil charges, trials, and in some cases, prison sentences.

The procedure in the **25th Amendment** for a president who is unable to perform his duties includes a written declaration of that fact to be transmitted to the speaker of the House of Representatives and the president pro tempore of the Senate. There is no explanation for the type of resignation Nixon faced. His decision to send a brief statement the 9th of August to the Secretary of State established a precedent.

The Last Chapter

President Nixon died of a fatal stroke on April 22, 1994. He was buried next to his wife, who had died the year before, on the grounds of the home in which he was born in Yorba Linda, California. Former presidents Ford, Carter, Reagan and Bush were among those present for the impressive military funeral at the burial site.

Eulogies were given by the Reverend Billy Graham; Henry Kissinger, former Secretary of State under Nixon; Senator Bob Dole; Pete Wilson, the governor of California; and President Clinton. President Clinton asked that Richard Milhous Nixon be remembered in the light of his entire life.

THE DUTIES AND POWERS OF THE PRESIDENT

Presidents get the blame in bad times and the praise in good times. The truth of the matter is that all three branches of the federal government must stay within the framework of the roles defined for them by the Constitution.

Constitutional References

Article II, Sec. 2, Par. (1) and (2)
Article II, Sec. 3

What the president is authorized to do (that is not covered in other chapters):

As Commander in Chief of the Armed Forces the president can grant pardons and reprieves for offenses against the United States and commission all officers of the United States. The Constitution wanted to establish civilian supremacy over the military. For that reason Congress was instructed to appropriate money for the army just two years at a time, **(Sec. 8, Par. (12) of Article I).**

The president is our supreme representative around the world, and today needs to be a super salesman at home. We cannot expect other countries to have more regard for our chief executive than we ourselves are willing to demonstrate. What is being honored is the *Office of the Presidency*, not the person who fills that office.

The president is the final authority over numerous departments that assist him in looking after the welfare of the people and executing the laws made by Congress.

The president is called upon to express his ideas before Congress, the nation and the world. His annual *State of the Union* address is specifically referred to in **Article II, Sec. 3** of the Constitution. President Clinton's televised address, given in the House of Representatives, has included in his audience all members of Congress, the Supreme Court, the president's Cabinet, heads of the military and federal agencies, business leaders and other citizens.

The president, "on extraordinary Occasions", can convene both houses of Congress, and, in the case of severe disagreement between the two houses, adjourn them until he thinks the time is right for them to again go about their business. presidents have been known to call special sessions of Congress, but none has ever exercised the right to adjourn Congress.

Presidents, "with the Advice and Consent of the Senate", can make treaties (when 2/3rd of the Senate agree), appoint ambassadors, other public ministers and consuls, justices of the Supreme Court and all other officers of the United States not already provided for.

What the President is NOT authorized to do:

Intervene in the internal affairs of a state unless requested to do so by that state's authorities.

Make any laws or pass on the constitutionality of the laws.

Constitutional Reference

The 22nd Amendment

Section 1. No person shall be elected to the office of the President more than twice, and no person who has held the office of President, or acted as President, for more than two years of a term to which some other person was elected president shall be elected to the office of the President more than once. But this Article shall not apply to any person holding the office of president when this Article was proposed by the Congress, and shall not prevent any person who may be holding the office of president, or acting as president, during the term within which this Article becomes operative from holding the office of president or acting as president during the remainder of such term.

Section 2. This article shall be inoperative unless it shall have been ratified as an amendment to the Constitution by the legislatures of three-fourths of the several States within seven years from the date of its submission to the States by the Congress.

Roosevelt / Truman and the 22nd Amendment

The only thing we have to fear is fear itself.
Franklin D. Roosevelt

The buck stops here.
Harry S Truman

Harry Truman was president for all but three months of Franklin Roosevelt's fourth term and then was elected for a term of his own. This would have disqualified him for another term except for the fact that he was the president in office when Congress proposed the **22nd Amendment** on March 24, 1947, and was still in office when it was ratified four years later. He chose not to run again. The longest period a person can serve under the **22nd Amendment** is 10 years, which applies to every president since Harry Truman.

Franklin Roosevelt, the only president to be in office longer than two terms, was just beginning his fourth elected term when he died of a cerebral hemorrhage. America was still involved in WWII. No one knows how long he might have remained president had he lived. Over the years he demonstrated great skill in handling crises and was a remarkably active president in spite of the fact that, as an adult polio victim, he could only walk in leg braces and with a cane. Fortunately for the country, Harry Truman, Roosevelt's choice of running mate for his fourth term, successfully met the challenge created by his death.

Until the **22nd Amendment** no limit had been placed by the Constitution on the number of times a person could run for this office. George

Washington had set a two term example that others simply followed--all but one president, that is. You might have guessed, it was another Roosevelt.

President Theodore Roosevelt

Speak softly and carry a big stick.
Theodore Roosevelt

(The "big stick" was a strong U.S. Navy)

Theodore Roosevelt, better known as "Teddy", was our "environmentalist president" and cousin of Franklin Roosevelt. After having been president from 1901-1909, Teddy decided in 1912 to try for a third term. His own Republican party was backing the incumbent, President William Howard Taft, for a second term. An undaunted Teddy formed the Progressive party, which was soon referred to as the Bull Moose party. With voters split between Roosevelt and Taft, the election went to Democrat Woodrow Wilson, the president who steered us through WWI. Teddy considered his greatest accomplishment to be the construction of the Panama Canal.

The Way of Politics and Elections in America

Key Words and Phrases

to adjourn	break off; postpone
to convene	assemble; come together
to concur; concurrence	to agree in opinion; agreement
electors	any voters. This word is frequently used in the Constitution and does not always refer to the Electoral College. It can, as in the **17th Amendment, Par. (1),** indicate the general public that is qualified to vote.
to modify	make some changes
to supersede	take the place of

The Emergence of Political Parties

The Constitution says nothing about political parties. George Washington was of the opinion that they discouraged agreement. However, there have always been differences among the states which inevitably did lead to the development of political parties.

At the time the Constitution was being formed the most intense conflict was over the amount of power the central government and the states should have. Those who favored a strong central government rallied around Alexander Hamilton and became known as the Federalists. Supporters of states' rights gravitated to Thomas Jefferson and James Madison and were referred to as the anti-Federalists.

It was known that George Washington was inclined to support the views of Alexander Hamilton, but he was unanimously elected president both times he was in office without the leverage of a political party.

Our second president, John Adams, came into office under the Federalist banner. The Anti-Federalists had by that time adopted the name Democratic/Republican and were usually called Republicans. They later dropped the word Republican and became the Democratic Party we know today. Andrew Jackson was the first president to be called a Democrat.

Federalists were replaced by Whigs who succeeded in getting their presidential candidate in office four times, but were ultimately displaced by a new Republican Party. The first Republican presidential candidate in office was Abraham Lincoln.

During the Civil War the South was predominantly Democratic and the North primarily Republican. Democrats in the North who sided with the Union, such as President Andrew Johnson, combined with Republicans to form the Union Republican Party. After the war this party reverted to the name Republican, which they have called themselves ever since.

Republicans accused the Democrats of starting the Civil War, and Democrats have held the Republicans responsible for the stock market crash of 1929 and resulting great depression. The blame game is not a new concept; it has simply become elevated in our era to a fine art.

Beyond the Two-Party System

Party machinery became more powerful and varied as this nation grew in size and complexity. The Communist Party was outlawed because its central theme was so revolutionary. Others have flourished, but none seem to be able to defeat the Democrats or Republicans. Although Ross Perot's Reform Party got him on the ballot in '92 an '96, not even with his virtually unlimited financial support was he able to win a single state. But who are these liberals, moderates and conservatives?

What the Dictionaries Say

Liberals - uphold civil liberties as central in a free society; believe in the doctrine of progress through government reform and change in an orderly (evolutionary rather than revolutionary) way; are politically open-minded.

Conservatives - tend to try to preserve the existing order of things; are cautious; desirous of staying within a safe margin; don't encourage abrupt or radical change; favor private enterprise and freedom from government controls; have fixed political attitudes.

Moderates - support views, opinions or practices within reasonable limits; try to keep issues and situations from becoming too extreme; are willing to compromise; tend to have flexible political party relationships.

The Political Scale

Far Left-Liberals	***Center-Moderates***	***Far Right-Conservatives***
Democrats	Democrats Republicans	Republicans

There is no simple classification of any political party or its members but, generally speaking, Democrats are center and to the left and Republicans are center and right of center. On the other hand, a liberal Democrat under certain conditions could consider a particular moderate to be too conservative and conversely, a conservative Republican might decide that same moderate is too liberal.

---- and then there are those who would just say, "That's America!"

Voting for Members of Congress

Constitutional References

Article I, Sec. 2, Par. (1) - House of Representatives:

The House of Representatives shall be composed of Members chosen every second Year by the People of the several States,...

Article I, Sec. 3, Par. (1) - Senate: (See 17th Amendment)

The Senate of the United States shall be composed of two Senators from each State, chosen by the Legislature thereof, for six Years; and each Senator shall have one Vote.

Article I, Sec. 4, Par. (1) - Congress: (See 17th Amendment)

The Times, Places and Manner of holding Elections for Senators and Representatives, shall be prescribed in each State by the Legislature thereof; but the Congress may at any time by Law make or alter such Regulations, except as to the Places of chusing Senators.

17th Amendment, Par. (1) - Replaces Article I, Sec. 3, Par.(1) modifies last sentence of Article I, Sec. 4, Par. (1)

The Senate of the United States shall be composed of two Senators from each State, elected by the people thereof for six years; and each Senator shall have one vote.

We have always elected members of the House of Representatives by popular vote, but until the **17th Amendment** was ratified in 1913 the Senate was chosen by state legislatures as specified in the Connecticut Compromise. By the time the **17th Amendment** switched the voting of Senators to popular vote half of the states were already asking their voters to declare their senatorial preferences in party primaries.

Congress established the first Tuesday after the first Monday in November for the election of representatives specifying that it be by secret ballot. Congress has to continuously deal with legislation concerning candidate contributions and election fraud and corruption.

REVOLT OF THE STATES AND THE PEOPLE

NATIONAL ELECTION OF '92 - A presidential and congressional Democratic victory.

Following Colorado's lead, in the 1992 election 14 states passed laws limiting the number of terms their elected state and federal representatives could serve. The constitutionality of these new state laws became a topic for debate throughout the country.

Term limit advocates took the stand that states' rights should be the deciding factor. The laws only concerned the states involved and addressed a subject which the Constitution had never covered.

Opponents of federal term limit restrictions contended that the Constitution designated Congress as our lawmaking body, particularly concerning issues which involved more than one state. The presidential term limit **(The 22nd Amendment)** was cited in support of the argument that changes of this kind should be submitted to all of the states through the amendment process. Although members of Congress are elected by and for their respective states, *collectively* they affect the whole country.

MID-TERM ELECTION OF '94 - a whopping congressional victory for Republicans.

In the November, 1994 election the Republicans swept the field, securing leadership in both houses of Congress for the first time in 40 years.

More states voted for term limits, increasing the number of states in revolt on this issue to 23. Even Washington, DC favored the defectors in their local election. (DC doesn't vote for members of Congress.)

ENTER THE SUPREME COURT - the constitutionality of term limits.

The end of May, 1995 the Supreme Court rendered a 5 to 4 decision that it was unconstitutional for the state of Arkansas to limit federal congressional terms. By association this verdict overturned the term limit law as passed in all of the other states, but does not affect the amendment process. (See the ***10th Amendment*** concerning this decision.)

Vote of the Majority

Stephen Breyer

Ruth Bader Ginsburg

Anthony Kennedy

David Souter

John Paul Stevens

"A self-imposed restriction is contrary to the fundamental principle of our representative democracy, embodied in the Constitution, that the people should chose whom they please to govern them."

Justice John Paul Stevens

Vote of the Dissenters

Chief Justice William Rehnquist

Clarence Thomas

Sandra Day O'Conner

Antonin Scalia

"The Constitution is simply silent on this question. And where the Constitution is silent, it raises no bar to action by the States or the people."

Justice Clarence Thomas

Voting for the President

Constitutional References
(The Electoral College)

Article II, Sec. I, Par. (2) - Creating the Electors:

Each State shall appoint, in such Manner as the Legislature thereof may direct, a Number of Electors, equal to the whole Number of Senators and Representatives to which the State may be entitled in the Congress: but no Senator or Representative, or Person holding an Office of Trust or Profit under the United States (government), shall be appointed an Elector.

Article II, Sec. I, Par. (4) - Congress and the Electoral College:

The Congress may determine the Time of chusing the Electors, and the Day on which they shall give their Votes; which Day shall be the same throughout the United States.

Today these electors in all of the states and the District of Columbia are elected by voters on a statewide ticket. The only exception has been the state of Maine with two of its four electors (two members in the House and two in the Senate) elected by congressional districts.

The minimum number of electors for any state and the District of Columbia is three- a single member in the House and two senators. California, with 54 electors, heads the list of states constantly watched by presidential candidates.

Congress has chosen the first Tuesday after the first Monday in November, in the years in which there are presidential elections, for the states to select their electors. Electors meet where their state legislatures direct, which is usually in their state capitals, to cast their votes (one to each person). They can vote for anyone they choose, but normally go with their state.

Some of the states have requested that their electors go the way their states go in a presidential election. There is no way this request can be legally enforced, but it has not so far presented a problem for the states that have introduced it. This point is not covered in the Constitution.

America obviously supports the popular vote, but at the time the Constitution was written the small states backed away from that approach fearing their voices would never be heard. The Electoral College appeared to be the best solution.

The **12th Amendment** replaces **Article II, Sec. 1, Par. (3)** concerning Electoral College procedure. Parts of this procedure are now out of date. The growing influence of political party primaries has led to presidential candidates and their running mates being confirmed in national party conventions instead of by the Electoral College. This narrows the voting field for both the Electoral College and the public at large.

The 12th Amendment (1804) - The Electoral College at Work:

1. Electors meet in their states and vote by ballot for the president and vice president (who are now of the same party).
2. Electors make lists of all votes for the president and vice president which they sign, certify and transmit sealed to the president of the Senate of the United States.
3. The president of the Senate, in the presence of the Senate and House of Representatives, opens the certificates (the votes being counted by a member of each party from the House of Representatives) and after the official count proclaims the victors.
4. Provision has been made concerning procedure in case no person has a clear majority of the votes.

Copies of all Electoral College votes are sent to designated state and federal government officials. No one is legally a president or vice president elect until all Electoral College votes are counted.

Feeling as America does today, if the Electoral College vote should reverse a popular vote, we would probably pressure Congress to alter or eliminate the system. This has been proposed before without any action being taken. Until such time, we will continue our double-voting way... and may the best man (?) win!

The 1992 National Election

Presidential Candidate	Political Party	Popular Vote Nov. 3, 1992	Electoral Vote Dec. 14, 1992
Bill Clinton	Dem.	43% - 32 states	370
George Bush	Rep.	38% - 18 states	168
Ross Perot	Reform	19% - 0 states	0

Bill Clinton needed 270 electoral votes to win.
The Electoral College had 535 state votes and 3 DC votes.

MORE FIRSTS FOR ELECTION '92

President Bill Clinton of Arkansas and *Vice President Al Gore* of Tennessee --- first southern presidential team since the reconstruction --- both born after WWII (in their 40's) --- Gore the first Vietnam War veteran in either the office of president or vice president.

Hillary Rodham Clinton --- the first president's wife with an educational degree beyond a four year college or university --- a law partner in a prominent Arkansas law firm.

Janet Reno --- President Clinton choice --- first woman Attorney General of the Justice Department.

Barbara Boxer (D) and *Dianne Feinstein* (D) of California ---the first two female senators ever elected in that or any other state.

Carol Moseley Braun (D) of Illinois --- the first African-American in the Senate, and *Patty Murray* (D) of Washington State, brought the total number of women senators up to six.

Ben Nighthorse Campbell (D) of Colorado --- Cheyenne Indian Chief, the only native American in the Senate since Kaw Indian *Charles Curtis* (R) of Kansas who became vice president in the Hoover Administration.

(Campbell, originally a Democrat, switched in 1995 to the Republican Party.)

The Lame-Duck Amendment

The **20th Amendment**, better known as the **Lame-Duck Amendment**, changed the times that the president and Congress adjourn and convene in order to lessen the transitional confusion and delay in the governing process. **Article I, Sec. 4, Par. (2)** of the Constitution had established the first Monday in December as the starting date for Congress, but the **20th Amendment, Sec. 1** is the first constitutional reference to a specific date for the president.

In the last paragraph of the body of the Constitution (a section not always published) that follows delegate signatures, the last sentence simply urges Congress and the president to "without Delay, proceed to execute this Constitution."

Following the instructions established in the Constitution, George Washington's first inauguration took place in New York City on April 30, 1789; his second, in Philadelphia on March 4, 1793, established a precedent that was followed until the **20th Amendment** was ratified. (President Washington took office before the last two states had ratified the Constitution - North Carolina in November, 1789 and Rhode Island in May, 1790.)

The "Lame-ducks" were a president or any members of Congress who had been defeated in a November election and had to stay on the job until the winners would be officially put in office on March 4.

THE LAST NATIONAL ELECTION OF THE 20TH CENTURY

NOVEMBER 5, 1996

Constitutional Reference

The 20th Amendment, Sec. 1 (1933)
Replaces Article I, Sec. 4,Par. (2)

Section 1. The terms of the President and Vice President shall end at noon on the 20th day of January, and the terms of Senators and Representatives at noon on the 3rd day of January, of the years in which such terms would have ended if this article had not been ratified; and the terms of their successors shall then begin.

The 1996 National Election

Presidential Candidate	Political Party	Popular Vote	Electoral Vote
Bill Clinton	Dem.	50% - 31 states	379
Bob Dole	Rep.	41% - 19 states	159
Ross Perot	Reform	9% - 0 states	0

Bill Clinton became the first democrat to be a two-term president since Franklin Roosevelt Although, this time he lost Colorado, Montana and Georgia, he gained Arizona and Florida. This shift gave him nine more Electoral College Votes and 7% more popular votes than he received in 1992. His Electoral Votes again included Washington, DC.

Bob Dole made no plans beyond the election. He wasn't used to being out of a job. Not so Republican Senator Strom Thurmond of South Carolina. The senator was reelected, as usual, and would, when this latest term expired, be 100 years old.

Ross Perot lost ground in and out of his Reform Party. Undaunted, he stated that he intended to remain politically active.

Electoral College Votes '96 Election

Bill Clinton

Arizona	8	Missouri	11
Arkansas	6	Nevada	4
California	54	New Hampshire	4
Connecticut	8	New Jersey	15
Delaware	3	New Mexico	5
Florida	25	New York	33
Hawaii	4	Ohio	21
Illinois	22	Oregon	7
Iowa	7	Pennsylvania	23
Kentucky	8	Rhode Island	4
Louisiana	9	Tennessee	11
Maine	4	Vermont	3
Maryland	10	Washington State	11
Massachusetts	12	West Virginia	5
Michigan	18	Wisconsin	11
Minnesota	10	Washington DC	3
		Total Electoral Votes	**379**

Bob Dole

Alabama	9	North Carolina	14
Alaska	3	North Dakota	3
Colorado	8	Oklahoma	8
Georgia	13	South Carolina	8
Idaho	4	South Dakota	3
Indiana	12	Texas	32
Kansas	6	Utah	5
Mississippi	7	Virginia	13
Montana	3	Wyoming	3
Nebraska	5	**Total Electoral Votes**	**159**

Congress was slightly realigned. A number of House of Representatives votes were so close it took weeks to get an accurate count. Republicans lost some of their freshmen who had supported the "Contract with America" in 1995. In the Senate, the Republican gain of one seat changed the ratio for the 105th Congress to 55 Republicans and 45 Democrats in that house. (House of Representative figures were still not available when this was written.) Republicans did retain a majority in both houses and became the first Republican dominated Congress to be reelected in over 60 years.

America produced no local or national tidal waves in the '96 election. The country seemed to be satisfied to settle for the balance of power provided by a Democratic president and Republican Congress. For the remaining years of the 20th Century the two major political parties would be watching each other, and America would be watching both of them. (See *Congress and the States* concerning the election of governors.)

Odds and Ends

THE INS AND OUTS OF PRESIDENT GROVER CLEVELAND

Grover Cleveland (D), president from 1885-1889, lost his bid for a second term to Benjamin Harrison (R) who was president from 1889-1893. When the next election time came around, Harrison found himself face to face with Grover Cleveland again. This time Cleveland won and become our 24th president after having been our 22nd president.

Grover Cleveland's success in getting elected for two non-consecutive terms is not unconstitutional, but no one else has accomplished it. In Cleveland's first bid against Harrison he won the popular vote, but lost the electoral vote. He remained a popular enough figure to succeed on his second try four years later.

The Supreme Court

The Judicial Branch that Interprets the Laws

If there is any fixed star in our constitutional constellation, it is that no official, high or petty, can prescribe what shall be orthodox in politics, nationalism, religion or other matters of opinion or force citizens to confess by word or act their faith therein.

Justice Robert H. Jackson
West Virginia Board of Education v Barnette (1943)
U.S. Supreme Court

THE UNITED STATES JUDICIAL SYSTEM

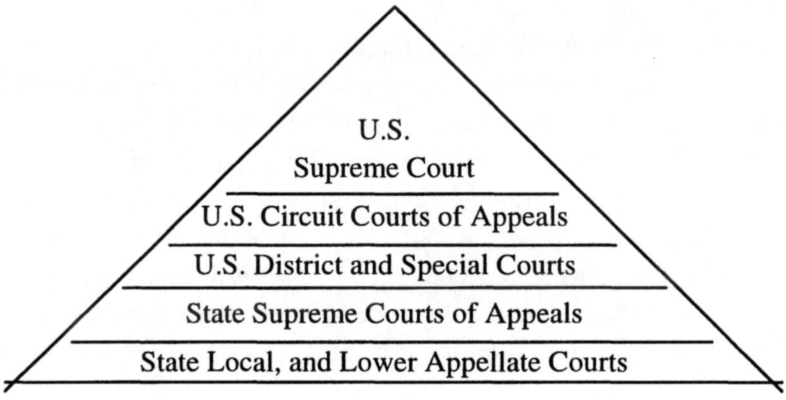

This chapter centers around our federal court system in general and U.S. Supreme Court in particular. State courts are not covered in the Constitution. They have been left in the hands of the states.

CONGRESS AND THE FEDERAL COURTS

Constitutional References

Article I, Sec. 8, Par. (9)

> The Congress shall have power --- To constitute Tribunals inferior to the supreme Court;

This article gives Congress authority over all federal courts except the Supreme Court.

Article III, Sec. 1

> The judicial Power of the United States, shall be vested in one supreme Court, and in such inferior Courts as the Congress may from time to time ordain and establish. The Judges, both of the supreme and inferior Courts, shall hold their Offices during good Behavior,...

The phrase "inferior courts" simply means those that have less authority than the Supreme Court. **Article III, Sec. 1** leaves no doubt that the Supreme Court, the only court specified in the Constitution, is the highest court of law in the United States. Holding office "during good Behavior" is another way of saying Court appointments are for life.

Judiciary "good Behavior" appointments were designed to lessen the possibility of political manipulation of judges and justices, but opened the door for congressional impeachments. Congress has at times removed judges by the impeachment process. And in 1805 Supreme Court Justice Samuel Chase was impeached, but was not convicted (Not Chief Samuel P. Chase of Ohio, who presided over President Johnson's impeachment trial in 1868). Although some Supreme Court justices have resigned under pressure, none have ever been forcefully removed from office.

A sufficient number of federal district courts have been created by acts of Congress to provide each state with at least one. There are also district courts for the District of Columbia and U.S. territories where applicable. The court of the Commonwealth of Puerto Rico is comparable to those in the states.

In the Circuit Court of Appeals Act of 1891, Congress established a relatively small number of circuit appeals courts to relieve the case load pressure on the Supreme Court. All of the states, the District of Columbia and territories as deemed necessary are attached to one of these circuits. For example, the Court of Appeals for the Federal Circuit in Washington, DC handles appeals from all federal courts involving specialized courts and agencies such as the Court of Military Appeals, International Trade, Claims, the U.S. Tax Court and the Patent Office.

Congress determines the number and kind of federal courts in the country and is responsible for the number of justices on the Supreme Court. In the period in which George Washington was president the Court had six justices. As president, Washington made eleven Supreme Court appointments in eight years, three of which were chief justice appointments. Many early justices, all of whom had been important revolutionary figures, chose not to remain long in this office.

Congress had originally, in the Judiciary Act of 1789, made six the official number of justices on the Supreme Court; the Judiciary Act of 1807 changed that number to seven; in the Judiciary Act of 1863, the number was increased to ten; a final adjustment was made in 1869 to nine justices, which has been the number ever since. The main reason for these changes was an attempt to arrive at the best balance for the Court's case load. However, politics does play a part. When Thomas Jefferson became president there was a vacancy on the Court. A hostile Congress reduced the legal number of justices to five to prevent the president from making an appointment. Under pressure, Congress restored the original number which was six.

THE PRESIDENT AND THE FEDERAL COURTS

Constitutional Reference

Article II, Sec. 2, Par. (2)

The President shall --- nominate, and by and with the Advice and Consent of the Senate, shall appoint Ambassadors, other public Ministers and Consuls, Judges of the supreme Court, and all other Officers of the United States, whose Appointments are not herein otherwise provided for, and which shall be established by Law: but the Congress may by Law vest the Appointment of such inferior Officers, as they think proper, in the President alone, in the Courts of Law, or in the Heads of Departments.

How political is our federal court system? Impeachment convictions are rare. As of 1995 only six U.S. district judges and one U.S. Commerce Court associate judge have been removed from office by Impeachment. It is unpredictable in the final analysis how judges or justices will conduct themselves and interpret cases presented to them. Some justices have become more liberal and others more conservative when they reached the Supreme Court.

Presidential Supreme Court Appointments
(The symbol "CJ" stands for Chief Justice)

Washington	8 + 3 CJ	Cleveland	3 + 1 CJ
J. Adams	2 + 1 CJ	McKinley	1
Jefferson	3	T. Roosevelt	3
Madison	2	Taft	5 + 1 CJ
Monroe	1	Wilson	3
J.Q. Adams	1	Harding	3 + 1 CJ
Jackson	4 + 1 CJ	Coolidge	1
Van Buren	3	Hoover -	2 + 1 CJ
Tyler	1	F. Roosevelt	8 + 1 CJ

Polk	2	Truman	3 + 1 CJ
Fillmore	1	Eisenhower	4 + 1 CJ
Pierce	1	Kennedy	2
Buchanan -	1	L. Johnson	2
Lincoln	4 + 1 CJ	Nixon	3 + 1 CJ
Grant	3 + 1 CJ	Ford	1
Hayes -	2	Reagan	3 + 1 CJ
Garfield	1	Bush	2
Arthur	2	Clinton	2
Harrison	4	(through Justice Stephen Breyer, the 97th Associate Justice on the Court)	

Composition of the Supreme Court

Chief Justice William Hubbs Rehnquist - Reagan appointment, 1986.

Born: October 1, 1924, Milwaukee, Wisconsin.

Education: Stanford and Harvard Universities; law degree Stanford Law School.

Experience: Law clerk to U.S. Supreme Court Justice Robert H. Jackson; private law practice, Phoenix, Arizona; U.S. assistant attorney general, Office of Legal Counsel; Nixon Supreme Court associate justice appointment, 1972. Decisions usually very conservative.

Associate Justices

Stephen Gould Breyer - Clinton appointment, 1994.

Born: August 15, 1938, San Francisco, California.

Education: Stanford University; Marshall Scholar, Oxford University, England; law degree Harvard Law School.

Experience: Law clerk to Supreme Court Justice Arthur J. Goldberg; special assistant (anti-trust) to Attorney General, U.S. Justice Department; professor, Harvard University and assistant professor, Harvard Law School; assistant special prosecutor Watergate Special Prosecution Force, U.S. Justice Department; Chief Counsel, Senate Judiciary Committee; Judge, 1980-1990, and Chief Judge, 1990-1994, First U.S. Circuit Court of Appeals, Boston. Considered to be a consensus builder.

Ruth Bader Ginsburg - Clinton appointment, 1993. Second female on the Supreme Court.

Born: March 15, 1933, Brooklyn, New York.

Education: Cornell University, Harvard and Columbia Law Schools.

Experience: Professor at Rutgers University Law School; first woman ever granted tenure as a professor at Columbia University Law School; as a supporter of women's rights, argued six landmark cases before the U.S. Supreme Court that forced a change in several state and federal laws discriminating against gender; Carter appointment to the District of Columbia Circuit Court of Appeals, 1980. Quoted as saying she is for evolutionary, not revolutionary change in the justice system. Usually votes with the majority.

Anthony McLeod Kennedy - Reagan appointment, 1988.

Born: July 23, 1936, Sacramento, California.

Education: London School of Economics; Stanford University; Harvard Law School.

Experience: Private law practice San Francisco and Sacramento; instructor of constitutional law, University of the Pacific; Ford appointment to the U.S. Court of Appeals, Ninth Circuit, 1975. His Supreme Court decisions are moderate to conservative.

Sandra Day O'Connor - Reagan appointment, 1981. First female on the Supreme Court.

Born: March 26, 1930, El Paso, Texas.

Education: Stanford University; Stanford Law School.

Experience: In Arizona: private practice; assistant attorney general; state senator; state superior court judge. In 1979, governor appointment to the Arizona Court of Appeals. In matters of religion, appears to favor a neutral government.

Antonin Scalia - Reagan appointment, 1986. Son of a Catholic Sicilian immigrant who became a language instructor at Brooklyn College.

Born: March 11, 1936, Trenton, New Jersey.

Education: Georgetown University; University of Fribourg, Switzerland; Harvard Law School.

Experience: Law practice Cleveland, Ohio; instructor at Georgetown, Universities of Virginia, Chicago and Stanford. Reagan appointment to the U.S. Circuit Court of Appeals for the District of Columbia. Considered to be one of the most conservative members on the Supreme Court.

David Hackett Souter - Bush appointment, 1990.

Born: September 17, 1939, Melrose, Massachusetts.

Education: Rhodes Scholar, Oxford University, England; Harvard University and Harvard Law School.

Experience: In New Hampshire: state assistant attorney general; judge in the state's Superior Court and Supreme Court; Bush appointment U.S. Court of Appeals, First Circuit, in July, 1990, and U.S. Supreme Court three months later. Believed to be a strict interpreter of the Constitution, but some Supreme Court decisions have been moderately liberal.

John Paul Stevens - Ford appointment, 1975.

Born: April 20, 1920, Chicago, Illinois.

Education: University of Chicago; Northwestern University School of Law.

Experience: Law clerk to Supreme Court Justice Wiley B. Rutledge; private practice, Chicago; associate counsel, sub-committee on the study of monopoly power, U.S. House of Representatives Judiciary Committee; member U.S. Attorney General's National Committee to Study the Anti-trust Laws; part-time instructor Northwestern and Chicago University Law Schools; judge, U.S. Court of Appeals, Seventh Circuit, Chicago. An independent voter in the Supreme Court, but usually moderate.

Clarence Thomas - Bush appointment, 1991. The second African-American on the Supreme Court.

Born: June 23, 1948, near Savannah, Georgia.

Education: Holy Cross and Yale Law School.

Experience: Includes private practice; state and federal positions include assistant attorney general for the state of Missouri; assistant secretary for civil rights, U.S. Department of Education; chairman of the Equal Employment Opportunity Commission; Bush appointment to the District of Columbia Circuit Court of Appeals, 1989. More conservative than his African-American predecessor, Thurgood Marshall, a Johnson appointment to the Supreme Court in 1967, who retired in 1991.

Over the years Thurgood Marshall and Ruth Bader Ginsburg, as litigators, have made more impact on state and federal laws than any other members of the Supreme Court.

About the Chief Justice

There is nothing in the Constitution or otherwise written that would prevent any justices from becoming involved in activities outside of the main arena of the Supreme Court if that is their choice. However, justices have from time to time been criticized for taking on too many additional tasks.

Congress has specified some of the activities of the Chief Justice. He has functioned as chairman of the Judicial Conference of the United States and Board of the Federal Judicial Center; supervisor of the Administrative Office of the United States Courts; a member of the Board of Regents of the Smithsonian Institution, the Board of Trustees of the National Gallery of Art, and the Joseph H. Hirshhorn Museum and Sculpture Garden.

THE MARSHALL ERA

Chief Justice John Marshall of Virginia, on the Supreme Court from 1801-1835 was the primary founder of the American system of constitutional law. He participated in more than 1,000 Supreme Court decisions and established the basic framework of the Supreme Court. He held this office until his death.

It is said than when John Marshall died (he was almost 80 years old) the Liberty Bell tolling his mourning cracked.

Judicial Self-Restraint

So little was covered in the Constitution about the Supreme Court it remained for the Court itself to work out procedures and areas of responsibility.

The Supreme Court established itself as the court of last resort whose official opinions would be confined to and expressed in the cases voluntarily brought to it. This was a remarkably advanced legal position for that period in history.

Judicial Immunity

From the start Supreme Court justices have had judicial immunity and cannot be sued for their *official* actions. A somewhat modified version applies to judges of the lower courts.

Judicial Review

In *Marbury v Madison (1803)* the Marshall Court defined what became known as judicial review, which established the right of the Supreme Court to review the acts of Congress. The Court struck down 105 congressional acts established by Congress between September 24, 1789 - February 7, 1972 that were declared unconstitutional in whole or in part. This judicial right was also extended to lower court judges. Judicial review has been based on the supremacy of the Constitution and has never been seriously challenged.

Implied and Enumerated Powers

Another Marshall Court decision, *McCulloch v Maryland (1819)* upheld the implied powers of Congress in **Article I, Sec. 8, Par. (18)** that granted Congress the power:

> To make all Laws which shall be necessary and proper for carrying into Execution the foregoing Powers, and all other Powers vested by this Constitution in the Government of the United States, or in any Department or Officer thereof.

In other words, Congress was not to be confined to the framework of enumerated powers (those specified in the Constitution) when a broader interpretation was required in order to carry out a power already specifically granted in the Constitution. For example, one of the enumerated powers of Congress is its right to "raise and support" an army and navy. This, by implication, gives it the power to establish additional branches of the Armed Forces as needed.

Inherent Powers

Marshall enforced the concept of inherent powers, those in the area of foreign affairs that the Court declared have existed for all governments whether or not they are covered in a Constitution - making war or negotiating treaties, developing diplomatic relations with other countries or exploring and claiming territory. Antarctica is an exploration example that the U.S. and many other countries have for years been peacefully undertaking.

Resulting Powers

The Supreme Court also recognizes that under certain conditions the combining of several enumerated powers can result in a new power acceptable under the Constitution. (Concurrent powers are covered under *Congress and the States.)*

The Constitution, making allowance for the language of the period in which it was written, is relatively simple. Many who helped create it had no legal background. What makes it complex is the interpretation of how it applies to each individual situation. It was not intended to be rigid. It was intended to reflect as well as guide America. For this reason we definitely need a *supreme* court to help us preserve both the spirit and the letter of this remarkable document.

THE SUPREME COURT ON THE JOB

Schedule of the Supreme Court

By law the Court convenes every year on the first Monday in October and adjourns in late June or July when the last case scheduled in concluded.

On rare occasions the Court holds a special session after adjournment to take care of urgent matters that are unable to be postponed. Such a case was *United States v Nixon.* On July 24, 1974 the Court unanimously denied that President Richard Nixon had the right under executive privilege to withhold documents the Watergate Special Prosecutor was requesting. The Court also in a special session struck down the Nixon Administration effort to keep the Pentagon Papers from being published.

SUPREME COURT CASES

Constitutional References

Article III, Sec. 2, Par. (1) - Appellate Jurisdiction
Article III, Sec. 2, Par. (2) - Original Jurisdiction

The Supreme Court has original jurisdiction, meaning lower federal courts are bypassed, when a case concerns a state, ambassadors, other public ministers or consuls. All other cases are on appeal from a lower court. Congress has a hand in the selection of appeal cases brought before the Supreme Court.

11th Amendment (1795)
Modifies Article III, Sec. 2, Par. (1)

> The Judicial power of the United States shall not be construed to extend to any suit in law or equity, commenced or prosecuted against one of the United States by Citizens of another State, or by Citizens or Subjects of any Foreign State.

The 11th Amendment was designed to reduce the power of federal courts by denying them the right to decide suits against states brought on by citizens of another state or citizens of a foreign state.

Interpretation has been complex. The states, Congress and the Supreme Court have all been known to make exceptions. Anyone affected by this amendment is advised to obtain a lawyer well versed in constitutional law and relevant court decisions.

Brandeis Rules of Restraint

Ashwander v Tennessee Valley Authority (1938) prompted Supreme Court Justice Louis D. Brandeis to put in writing the guidelines of the Court in case selection. (These are suggested, not mandatory rules.)

1. The Court does not pass on the constitutionality of cases that are non-adversarial, there must be real controversy. The Supreme Court is the Court of last resort.
2. The Court does not choose to "anticipate a question of constitutional law" before it is absolutely necessary to a case decision.
3. The Court will not "formulate a rule of constitutional law" broader than its specific application to the case in hand.
4. The Court prefers not to pass on the constitutionality of a case if it can be resolved another way. Wherever possible the Court decides a case on the basis of general law rather than constitutional law.
5. The Court will not pass on the validity of a statute a person is challenging if that person cannot demonstrate personal injury under the statute.
6. The Court will not pass on the constitutionality of a statute if the person requesting that it be considered constitutional profited from it.
7. Concerning the review of congressional acts, it is a "cardinal principle" of the court to first make sure that no possible constitutional interpretation can be found in the Constitution before declaring any congressional act unconstitutional.

Justice Jackson's "Fixed Star" in Our Constitutional Constellation

Constitutional References

Article II, Sec. 1, Par. (8) - Presidential Oath of Office:

I do solemnly swear (or affirm) that I will faithfully execute the Office of President of the United States,...

Article VI, Sec. 3 - Oath of Office, All State and Federal Government Officials:

The Senators and Representatives---, and the Members of the several State Legislatures, and all executive and judicial Officers, both of the United States and of the several States,

> shall be bound by Oath or Affirmation, to support this Constitution; but no religious Test shall ever be required as a Qualification to any Office or public Trust under the United States.

The president and all government officials are given a choice between "swear" and "affirm" becuase it is against some people's religion to swear. A person's religion does not present an obstacle to holding a government office.

14TH Amendment, Sec. 1 (1868) - Citizen Privileges, Immunities and Protection:

> No State shall make or enforce any law which shall abridge the privileges or immunities of citizens of the United States --- nor deny to any person within its jurisdiction the equal protection of the laws.

1st Amendment (1791) - Freedom of Religion:

> Congress shall make no law respecting an establishment of religion, or prohibiting the free exercise thereof;

In the area of religion, this federal government wanted to see religion of the people's choice flourish. The Founding Fathers, for the most part, were religious. When George Washington took his Oath of Office as president he added the statement, "so help me God", and kissed the Bible.

What the Founders wanted to prevent was the centuries of senseless killings and tortures, many times sponsored by governments, for the purpose of having a particular faith prevail exclusively.

The Bill of Rights was originally designed to keep the federal government from interfering with the rights of the states and the people. After the Civil War and ratification of the **14th Amendment**, many parts of the Bill of Rights, including the **1st Amendment**, became the responsibility of the states as well as the federal government concerning the rights of the people. It was not possible for the federal government to remain silent. Public schools, for instance, are state government institutions that are also recipients of federal government aid when it is requested by a state.

Supreme Court Justice Owen J. Roberts in *Cantwell v Connecticut (1940)* aptly defined the government dilemma over the **1st Amendment**:

> "... the First Amendment embraces two concepts - *freedom to believe and freedom to act.* The first is absolute but, in the nature of things, the second cannot be (absolute)."

It is an unfortunate fact that from time to time violence erupts in this country over the very rights that the Constitution established in the first place to try to give every American citizen equal access to those rights.

Odds and Ends

Have We Always Had An Income Tax?

Article I, Sec. 9, Par. (4)

No Capitation, or other direct, Tax shall be laid, unless in Proportion to the Census or Enumeration herein before directed to be taken.

The 16th Amendment - Replaces Article I, Sec. 9, Par. (4)

The Congress shall have power to lay and collect taxes on incomes, from whatever source derived, without apportionment among the several States, and without regard to any census or enumeration.

During the Civil War Congress levied an income tax to help finance the war for the Union. The Supreme Court upheld the decision, but after the war, struck down the tax on the grounds that in normal times it should be arrived at by consent of the states. Income tax was not introduced again until the 16th Amendment was ratified in 1913.

Congress and the States

> The powers not delegated to the United States (government) by the Constitution, nor prohibited by it to the States, are reserved to the States respectively, or to the people.
>
> **10th Amendment**
> U.S. Constitution

Constitutional Reference

Article I, Sec. 8, Par. (3) - Commercial Powers of Congress:

The Congress shall have Power --- To regulate Commerce with foreign Nations, and among the several States, and with the Indian Tribes;

It is through *Article I, Sec. 8, Par. (3)* that Congress gained control of Indian affairs. The commerce clause gives Congress tremendous power. So what does that leave the states?

Unlike the central government, which is specifically told what it can and cannot do by the Constitution, the states are free to make any decisions that are *not* in violation of the Constitution. In other words, the Constitution only tells the states what *not* to do.

Basically each state takes care of its own affairs and Congress handles matters that concern more than one state. This protects states from being overridden by other states as well as by the central government.

Article I, Sec. 10, Par. (1) - Restrictions on the States:

No State shall ---

Par. (1) --- enter into any Treaty, Alliance or Confederation;
(The states must not invade the territory of the federal government in the matter of foreign affairs.)

Par. (1) --- grant Letters of Marque and Reprisal;
(This practice, primarily of royalty, granting subjects the right to prey on enemy shipping, was outlawed in the mid 1800's.)

Par. (1) --- coin Money; emit Bills of Credit; make any Thing but gold and silver Coin a Tender in Payment of Debts;
(The federal government has to be in charge of the currency system in order to keep it uniform throughout the country and control it's impact on this country and foreign markets.)

Par. (1) --- pass any Bill of Attainder, ex post facto Law, or Law impairing the Obligation of Contracts, or grant any Title of Nobility.
(The "Obligation of Contracts" concerns contracts made by the states as well as between individuals. Neither the states nor the federal government can grant titles of nobility.)

Articles I, Sec. 10, Par. (2) and (3)-Without Congress' Consent:

No State shall, without the Consent of the Congress,---

Par. (2) --- lay any Imposts or Duties on Imports or Exports, except what may be absolutely necessary for executing its inspection Laws: and the net Produce of all Duties and Imposts, laid by any State on Imports or Exports, shall be for the Use of the Treasury of the United States; and all such Laws shall be subject to the Revision and Controul of the Congress.

(This restriction was designed to prevent state interference in the right of Congress to regulate commerce with foreign nations.)

Par. (3) --- lay any Duty of Tonnage, keep Troops, or Ships of War in time of Peace, enter into any Agreement or Compact with another State, or with a foreign Power,
("Duty of Tonnage" relates to charging a vessel for entering or leaving a port or navigating public waters. Every state has the right to keep a Militia, but not a standing army or navy.)

Par. (3) or engage in War, unless actually invaded, or in such imminent Danger as will not admit of delay.

Article I, Sec. 9, Par. (5) and (6) - Restrictions on both the States and Congress:

Par. (5) No Tax or Duty shall be laid on Articles exported from any State.
(But Congress can, under its powers to regulate commerce with foreign nations, exact an embargo to stop the exportation of an article in question.)

Par. (6) No Preference shall be given by any Regulation of Commerce or Revenue to the Ports of one State over those of another: nor shall Vessels bound to, or from, one State be obliged to enter, clear, or pay Duties in another.

Article I, Sec. 8, Par. (16) - Working Together, the Militia:

The Congress shall have Power ---

Par. (16) To provide for organizing, arming, and disciplining, the Militia, and for governing such Part of them as may be employed in the Service of the United States, reserving to the States respectively, the Appointment of the Officers, and the Authority of training the Militia according to the discipline prescribed by Congress;
(When the National Guard, for example, is called into the service of the United States, it becomes a part of the U.S. military forces. For that

period of time it is under the command of the President, as Commander in Chief and Congress.)

Article IV, Sec. 1 - Working Together, Full Faith and Credit:

Full Faith and Credit shall be given in each State to the public Acts, Records, and judicial Proceedings of every other State. And the Congress may by general Laws prescribe the Manner in which such Acts, Records and Proceedings shall be proved, and the Effect thereof.

Highways and Bi-Ways - Concurrent Tax Power:

Intrastate highways, those that don't extend beyond the boundaries of a state, are the responsibility of that state. Interstate highways, which run through more than one state, involve the federal government. The main source of revenue is the tax on gasoline. This right to tax is an example of concurrent power - that residing with both the states and Congress.

Concerning commerce and all other activities, state governments are expected to enforce all state and federal laws that apply to them.

PROHIBITION

THE 18TH AMENDMENT (1919)

Section 1. After one year from the ratification of this article the manufacture, sale, or transportation of intoxicating liquors within, the importation thereof into, or the exportation thereof from the United States and all territory subject to the jurisdiction thereof for beverage purposes is hereby prohibited.

Section 2. The Congress and the several States shall have concurrent power to enforce this article by appropriate legislation.

Section 3. This article shall be inoperative unless it shall have been ratified as an amendment to the Constitution by the legislatures of the several States as provided in the Constitution, within seven years from the date of the submission hereof to the States by the Congress.

This amendment was proposed in 1917 during WWI and became law shortly after the war was over in January, 1919. It is the only amendment that specifically establishes concurrent federal and state enforcement power **(Section 2)**.

Prohibition created chaos throughout the country. It was such a deep invasion of people's private lives that many Americans simply ignored the law. It threw out legitimate businesses and ushered in the gangster era. The quality of the liquor was no longer being regulated and some caused severe physical damage, even death.

As the transition was being made people were going in and out from "wet" to "dry" states. For years people traveling on trains could only buy an alcoholic drink in the club car when the train was moving through a "wet" state. In that era it felt like we had no sooner gotten every state "dry" than we repealed the law and had to go through it all again.

The Repeal of Prohibition

THE 21ST AMENDMENT (1933)

> **Section 1.** The eighteenth article of amendment to the Constitution of the United States is hereby repealed.
>
> **Section 2.** The transportation or importation into any State, Territory, or possession of the United States for delivery or use therein of intoxicating liquors, in violation of the laws thereof, is hereby prohibited.
>
> **Section 3.** This article shall be inoperative unless it shall have been ratified as an amendment to the Constitution by conventions in the several States, as provided in the Constitution, within seven years from the date of the submission hereof to the States by the Congress.

The **21st Amendment**, after it was proposed in February of 1933, took less than a year to repeal the **18th Amendment**.

This time Congress requested that the repeal amendment be acted on by state conventions **(Section 3)**, not state legislatures as requested in the **18th Amendment**. It was left to individual states to decide if they wanted to be "dry" or "wet". **Section 2** was designed to cover any state that wished to remain "dry." This approach comes closer to meeting the desires of the American people.

The **21st Amendment** has increased state authority in the area of commerce. However, Congress has the right to interfere if it believes a state is interpreting this amendment too loosely. State authority is designed to cover alcoholic beverages only.

America decided that it is the *abuse* rather than the *use* of alcohol that needed to be addressed; also adequate help provided for alcoholics whose special problem an amendment was unable to cure.

STATE GOVERNORS

(As of the November, 1994, mid-term election)

State	Governor	Party	Term Expires
Alabama	Fob James, Jr.	R	Jan. 1999
Alaska	Tony Knowles	D	Dec. 1998
Arizona	Fife Symington	R	Jan. 1999
Arkansas	Jim Guy Tucker	D	Jan. 1999
California	Pete Wilson	R	Jan. 1999
Colorado	Roy Romer	D	Jan. 1999
Connecticut	John G. Rowland	R	Jan. 1999
Delaware	Thomas R. Carper	D	Jan. 1997
Florida	Lawton Chiles	D	Jan. 1999
Georgia	Zell Miller	D	Jan. 1999
Hawaii	Benjamin J. Cayetano	D	Dec. 1998
Idaho	Philip E. Batt	R	Jan. 1999
Illinois	Jim Edgar	R	Jan. 1999
Indiana	Evan Bayh	D	Jan. 1997

Table (Continued)

State	Governor	Party	Term Expires
Iowa	Terry E. Branstad	R	Jan. 1999
Kansas	Bill Graves	R	Jan. 1999

Kentucky	Brereton C. Jones	D	Dec. 1995
Louisiana	Edwin W. Edwards	D	Jan. 1996
Maine*	Angus S. King Jr.	Ind	Jan. 1999
Maryland	Parris N. Glendening	D	Jan. 1999
Massachusetts	William F. Weld	R	Jan. 1999
Michigan	John Engler	R	Jan. 1999
Minnesota	Arne H. Carlson	R	Jan. 1999
Mississippi	Kirk Fordice	R	Jan. 1996
Missouri	Mel Carnahan	D	Jan. 1997
Montana	Marc Racicot	R	Jan. 1997
Nebraska	E. Benjamin Nelson	D	Jan. 1999
Nevada	Robert J. Miller	D	Jan. 1999
New Hampshire*	Stephen Merrill	R	Jan. 1997
New Jersey	Christine Todd Whitman	R	Jan. 1998
New Mexico	Gary E. Johnson	R	Jan. 1999
New York	George E. Pataki	R	Jan. 1999
North Carolina	James B. Hunt, Jr.	D	Jan. 1997
North Dakota	Edward T. Schafer	R	Jan. 1997
Ohio	George V. Voinovich	R	Jan. 1999
Oklahoma	Frank Keating	R	Jan. 1999
Oregon	John A. Kitzhaber	D	Jan. 1999
Pennsylvania	Tom Ridge	R	Jan. 1999
Rhode Island*	Lincoln C. Almond	R	Jan. 1999
South Carolina	David M. Beasley	R	Jan. 1999
South Dakota	William J. Janklow	R	Jan. 1999
Tennessee	Don Sundquist	R	Jan. 1999
Texas	George W. Bush Jr.	R	Jan. 1999

Table (Continued)

State	Governor	Party	Term Expires
Utah	Michael O. Leavitt	R	Jan. 1997
Vermont*	Howard Dean	D	Jan. 1997
Virginia	George F. Allen	R	Jan. 1998
Washington	Mike Lowry	D	Jan. 1997
West Virginia	Gaston Caperton	D	Jan. 1997
Wisconsin	Tommy G. Thompson	R	Jan. 1999
Wyoming	Jim Geringer	R	Jan. 1999

* Note: All terms for governor run 4 years except in the states of New Hampshire and Vermont which have 2 year terms for this office. As of 1996 the Rhode Island governor's office is a 4 instead of 2 year term. Maine supported a governor who is an Independent.

Various types of term limits for the governor's office have become part of some state constitutions, such as: (1) a person cannot serve a third consecutive term (which has been the most popular term restriction amont the states); (2) a person can only serve 2 terms - consecutive or otherwise; (3) cannot succeed oneself in office; (4) not eligible if in this office during 8 of the previous 14 years.

In the November, 1994 mid-term election Republicans emerged the winners at both the state and national level. Their number of state governors escalated to 30.

Governors began to press for more state control of funds allocated to the states by Congress (e.g., sums of money given with few, or preferably, no strings attached called block grants). Local governments, in turn, began asking for more authority concerning distribution of these funds by their state legislatures.

Some governors and mayors were taking a more cautious view of this large-scale transfer of responsibility. They felt that complex issues, such as reform of the welfare system, could result in mixed blessings for the states if not very carefully managed.

'95 Mid-term Election

Kentucky
Brerton C. Jones (D) could not by law run again. He was replaced by his lieutenant governor, Paul Patton (D).

Louisiana
Edwin W. Edwards (D) chose not to run a fifth term. His state turned to the Republican Party and elected former state senator Mike Foster ®.

Mississippi
Incumbent reelected.

'96 National Election

The governors of 11 states were affected by this election.
Incumbents reinstated:

Delaware	North Carolina
Missouri	North Dakota
Montana	Utah
Vermont	

Indiana
Evan Bayh (D) was replaced by his lieutenant governor, Frank O'Bannon (D).

New Hampshire
Democrat Jeanne Shaheen defeated Republican incumbent Stephen Merrill to become the first woman governor in that state.

Washington
Republican Cecil Underwood defeated Democrat Gaston Caperton.

Party Distribution of State Governors by 1977

31 Republicans

18 Democrats

1 Independent

Part III

We the People

Loyalty, Crime and the Constitution

> The Senators and Representatives --- and the Members of the several State Legislatures, and all executive and judicial Officers, both of the United States and of the several States, shall be bound by Oath or Affirmation, to support this Constitution;
>
> **Article VI, Par. (3)**
> U.S. Constitution

The Constitution and Congressional Conduct

The Constitution has given Congress more detailed direction than any other branch of the federal government. Congress not only has the responsibility of making the laws, but also the authority to police itself, and, through the impeachment process, remove government officials from office.

Concerning removal of congressional members, the general feeling has been that when a state becomes dissatisfied with the behavior of one of its elected members, if Congress does not expel that person, the situation can usually be dealt with in the next appropriate election.

To date no member of Congress has been removed by impeachment. In 1799 Senator William Blount-signer of the Constitution for the state of

North Carolina, and the first territorial governor of Tennessee- was impeached, but all charges were subsequently dropped.

Constitutional References

Article I, Sec. 5, Par. (1), (2) and (4)

Par. (1) Each House shall be the Judge of the Elections, Returns and Qualifications of its own Members, and a Majority of each (house) shall constitute a Quorum to do Business; but a smaller Number may adjourn from day to day, and may be authorized to compel the Attendance of absent Members, in such Manner, and under such Penalties as each House may provide.

Par. (2) Each House may determine the Rules of its Proceedings, punish its Members for disorderly Behavior, and, with the Concurrence of two thirds, expel a Member.

Par. (4) Neither House, during the Session of Congress, shall, without the Consent of the other, adjourn for more than three days, nor to any other Place than that in which the two Houses shall be sitting.

Today both houses may recess from time to time, but members of Congress are no longer part time employees and do not adjourn. However, these clauses do demonstrate the desire of those who created the Constitution to have the two houses function independently of each other and at the same time work together.

Article I, Sec. 6, Par. (1) and (2)

Par. (1) The Senators and Representatives --- shall in all Cases, except Treason, Felony and Breach of the Peace, (crimes in general) be privileged from Arrest during their Attendance at the Session of their respective Houses, and in going to and returning from the same; and for any Speech or Debate in either House, they shall not be questioned in any other Place.

Par. (2) No Senator or Representative shall, during the Time for which he was elected, be appointed to any civil Office under the Authority of the United States, which shall have been created, or the Emoluments whereof shall have been encreased during such time; and no Person holding any (other) Office under the United States, shall be a Member of either House during his Continuance in (that) Office.

Committees Related to Congressional Conduct

Congress functions through committees, several of which relate to congressional organization and the conduct of its members:

1. *Three Standing Committees of the House of Representatives*
   House Administration
   Rules Committee - Rules of the House
   Standards of Official Conduct

2. *Senate Standing Committee*
   Rules and Administration

3. *Select Senate Committee*
   Committee on Ethics

4. *Joint Committee (both Houses)*
   On the Organization of Congress

The Constitution and Treason

Constitutional Reference

Article III, Sec. 3, Par. (1) and (2)

Par. (1) Treason against the United States, shall consist only in levying War against them, or in adhering to their Enemies, giving them Aid and Comfort. No Person shall be convicted of Treason unless on the Testimony of two Witnesses to the same overt Act, or on Confession in open Court.

Par. (2) The Congress shall have Power to declare the Punishment of Treason, but no Attainder of Treason shall work Corruption of Blood, or Forfeiture except during the Life of the Person attainted.

It is indicated in **Par. (1)** that a person can either be accused of treason who engages in war against the United States or who gives the kind of "aid and comfort" that could promote the cause of a declared enemy.

The testimony of two witnesses is an important point. In this country, a person cannot be convicted of treason on circumstantial evidence alone. A confession in open court is sufficient evidence for conviction. In peace time it is not easy to identify and succeed in convicting a traitor

Par. (2) gives Congress the power to declare punishment for treason. The Constitution offers no guidelines concerning punishment except to outlaw an old custom that not only sentenced the traitor, but in a real sense could also sentence any family that person might have. Families of declared traitors had been known to be stripped of their titles, lands and all sources of income. The Constitution states that the penalty cannot include "Corruption of Blood or Forfeiture" or go beyond the "Life of the person attainted," the convicted traitor.

The Supreme Court has seldom reviewed charges of treason. Three WWII cases did ultimately reach the Court - *Cramer v Unites States (1945); Haupt v United States (1947); and Kawakita v United States (1952).* Very little discussion was added in one case and the other two left interpretation of part of the law in doubt.

THE CONSTITUTION AND "INSURRECTION OR REBELLION"

The phrase "Insurrection or Rebellion" is only used in the Constitution in **Sec. 3** and **Sec. 4** of the post-Civil War **14th Amendment**, and refers to the southern states that seceded from the United States. The Constitution remained silent throughout the war.

This section deals only with the effect of the Civil War on the states and federal government. The next chapter will cover the war's impact on the Constitution in the area of human rights.

The Civil War was about the institution of slavery, and it was about economics, politics, states' rights and defending one's turf.

To observe the ever increasing friction between the North and South - their differences in attitudes and customs, the competitiveness of their economies and political power in Washington - must have been like watching pressure build along an earthquake fault line, knowing that the day could come when a final thrust would shake the entire area with an intensity that would never be forgotten.

"Bleeding Kansas," the territory preparing for statehood, was being torn apart by pro-slavery and anti-slavery factions. Abraham Lincoln made the prophetic observation, "I do not expect the house to fall, but I do expect it will cease to be divided. It will become all one thing or all the other."

And then South Carolina, one of the creators of the United States Constitution, withdrew from the United States.

Time-table of the Break-up of the States

Fall of 1860:

Abraham Lincoln elected President of the United States.

December 20, 1860:

South Carolina left the Union.

January 9, 1861:

South Carolina fired on the steamer Star of the West. More states seceded:

January 9 -Mississippi	January 18 -Georgia
January 10 -Florida	January 26 -Louisiana
January 11 -Alabama	February 1 -Texas

February 18, 1861:

The Confederate States of America were formed in Montgomery, Alabama; Jefferson Davis, President.

March 4, 1861:

Inauguration of United States President Abraham Lincoln.

April 14, 1861:

Defeat of Fort Sumpter in Charleston, South Carolina, by South Carolina Militiamen. President Lincoln had not removed the armed Union force at Fort Sumpter or acknowledged the new Confederate government. More secessions followed:

April 17 -Virginia, the state that had given the United States seven presidents

May 6 - Arkansas

End of May - North Carolina

June 8 - Tennessee

Shortly after Arkansas voted for secession both northern and southern troops established governments in that state.

The border slave states of Delaware, Maryland, Kentucky and Missouri voted to stay in the Union.

Secessionists organized groups in Kentucky and Missouri that sent representatives to the Confederate Congress. (There are 13 stars in the Confederate flag.) At one point some secessionists declared Missouri to be in the Confederacy, but this action was not officially accepted. Both Missouri and Kentucky were occupied by Southern and Northern troops during the War.

Composition of the United States in the Civil War

22 states and all U.S. Territories remained a part of the United States, and the United States gained three new states:

January 29, 1861 - Kansas

June 20, 1863 - West Virginia

October 31, 1864 - Nevada

To Be Remembered

Three of the most important Civil War and Reconstruction personalities were from the South and never owned a slave:

Abraham Lincoln of Kentucky, who was assassinated; Robert E. Lee of Virginia, who lost his citizenship and never got it back in his lifetime; and Andrew Johnson of North Carolina, the only United States president to ever be impeached.

THE CONSTITUTION AND IMPEACHMENT

Constitutional References

Article I, Sec. 2, Par. (5) - House of Representatives:

> The House of Representatives --- shall have the sole Power of Impeachment.

Impeachment is just the first step. It is the House of Representatives that, after it is decides a person should be removed from office, organizes the case against the individual and presents it to the Senate for trial.

Article I, Sec. 3, Par. (6) - The Senate:

> The Senate shall have the sole Power to try all Impeachments. When sitting for that Purpose, they shall be on Oath or Affirmation. When the President of the United States is tried, the Chief Justice shall preside: And no Person shall be convicted without the concurrence of two thirds of the Members present. Judgement in Cases of Impeachment shall not extend further than to removal from Office, and disqualification to hold and enjoy any Office of honor, Trust or Profit under the United States: but the Party convicted shall nevertheless be liable and subject to Indictment, Trial, Judgement and Punishment, according to Law.

An impeachment conviction would under most circumstances involve serious enough charges for an indictment to follow, but that would not automatically be the case. Congress has no authority beyond removal from office.

Article II, Sec. 4 - All Civil Officers:

> The President, Vice President and all civil Officers of the United States, shall be removed from Office on Impeachment for, and Conviction of, Treason, Bribery, or other High Crimes and Misdemeanors.

This leaves a great deal of room for determining whether or not a government official is guilty of a serious enough violation to warrant removal from office in this manner. In normal times impeachments are rare. Not so in the climate in which Andrew Johnson was president.

The Impeachment of President Andrew Johnson

Background

Andrew Johnson was born in Raleigh, North Carolina, the son of a tavern handyman who died when his son was only three years old. Andrew had scant formal learning, but did receive some training as an apprentice to a Raleigh tailor. At the age of 16 he ran away from home. He prospered as a tailor and brought his mother and family to live with him when he settled in Greenville, Tennessee. Married at the age of 18, he soon began his remarkable political career - on the town council, the town mayor and then a state legislator.

Johnson was hard-driving, blunt and virtually humorless, but he instilled confidence in people. He became a member of the House of Representatives at the age of 33, and governor of Tennessee by the time he was 45. After serving two terms in that capacity, he represented his state in the Senate. When Tennessee seceded Johnson made his decision to stay in the Union. Although he had, as a Democrat, opposed Abraham Lincoln's presidential election, he was picked to be Lincoln's Union Republican running mate for his second term in office.

President Lincoln had said, "Blood cannot restore blood and government should not act for revenge." President Johnson tried against great odds to apply this philosophy to the reconstruction of the South.

Composition of the United States Senate

At the time of the Johnson impeachment there were 52 members representing 26 states in the Senate. (Nebraska had become a state on March 1, 1867.) None of the seceded states were represented. The Senate was dominated by radical Republicans.

Two acts had been passed over President Johnson's veto: The First Reconstruction Act, which put the defeated states under military rule, with strict laws laid down for readmission into the Union; and The Tenure of Office Act, requiring that the president have Senate approval before dismissing any presidential appointee who had originally been confirmed by the Senate.

President Johnson was not carrying out the Reconstruction Act to the satisfaction of Congress. He could see that it would work against freed slaves and defeated whites alike because of the total destruction of the economic base of the South. The conquered region was going to need constructive help in order to become stabilized enough to begin the monumental task of building a new way of life for everyone. (This was a lesson the United States still had not learned at the end of WWI in relation to the effective treatment of conquered people, but did apply to Japan and Germany after WWII.)

The move that galvanized Congress was Johnson's dismissal of his radical Secretary of War, Edwin M. Stanton, without consulting the Senate. This violation of the Tenure of Office Act gave Congress the opening it had been waiting for to remove President Johnson from office.

Impeachment and Trial

In February of 1868 the House of Representatives assembled and approved (by vote) the impeachment charges against President Andrew Johnson to be sent to the Senate. Chief Justice of the Supreme Court, Salmon P. Chase, was to preside over the Senate trial which began on March 13, 1868.

The Senate was going to need 36 votes (2/3rds of the Senate) to convict and Johnson needed 19 for an acquittal. The President had the support of 9 Democrats and 3 conservative Republicans. He had to have the votes of at least 7 of the 12 doubtful Republicans. Senator James Grimes of Iowa, who was paralyzed, had been brought in on a stretcher.

President Johnson's lawyers built a strong case against the Tenure of Office Act, declaring it was unconstitutional. The prosecution was using the President's dismissal of Stanton to demonstrate their most important charge that he was trying to obstruct Congress. When that charge was voted on there were 35 "guilty" and exactly 19 "not guilty" votes. The vote on the next two articles produced the same results. By that time the Senate moved to drop all charges and dismiss the trial.

Senator James Grimes, voting from his stretcher, had brought about the acquittal of the President of the United States.

Andrew Johnson's Last Years

President Johnson's term of office expired shortly after his impeachment trial and he returned to Tennessee. Six years later when Tennessee's statehood was restored, he reappeared on the Washington scene as a United States senator. Even those who worked against him during his presidential years had to admire his tenacity and courage.

The Constitution and the People

We the People of the United States,
in Order to form a more perfect Union,
establish Justice,
insure domestic Tranquility,
provide for the common defense,
promote the general Welfare,
and secure the Blessings of Liberty
to ourselves and our Posterity,
do ordain and establish this Constitution
for the United States of America.

The Preamble
U.S. Constitution

KEY WORDS AND PHRASES

bill of attainder

a paper authorizing that a person be stripped of all civil rights and/or personal possessions, what is known as being "dead in the law;" outlawed by the Constitution.

common law

taken from British law; unwritten law based on custom, usage and how like cases were determined in the past.

double jeopardy

prosecuted or punished more than once for the same offense; outlawed by the Constitution.

ex post facto law

a law that is retroactive and could penalize a person for action taken before the law went into effect; outlawed by the Constitution.

indentured servants

immigrants who contracted to work without pay for a specified period of time for people in this country who advanced them the amount of money needed to get here.

probable cause

a person cannot be arrested without solid evidence identifying the person as the one guilty of a specified crime for which arrested; arrest is a declaration of *probable* guilt, a jury will determine *actual* guilt.

to indict; an indictment

to charge with a crime; a formal written charge of a crime.

warrant

a judicial writ or order authorizing the arrest, search, seizure, or any other act designed to aid the administration of justice; legal backing for action taken.

writ of habeas corpus

Latin for "you have the body"; a legal paper (writ) commanding that a person being held be brought before the court or judge to determine if it is legal to hold that person.

RIGHTS OF THE PEOPLE - THE BODY OF THE CONSTITUTION

Although the body of the Constitution gives the most thought to the structure and function of the federal government and it's relation to the states, some important articles do specifically relate to the welfare of the people.

Article I, Sec. 8, Par. (4), (7) and (8) - Congressional Support:

"The Congress shall have Power To ---"

Par. (4) ---to establish an uniform Rule of Naturalization, and uniform Laws on the subject of Bankruptcies throughout the United States;

Par. (7) ---to establish Post Offices and post Roads;

Par. (8) ---to promote the Progress of Science and useful Arts, by securing for limited Times to Authors and Inventors the exclusive Right to their respective Writings and Discoveries;

Article I, Sec. 9, Par. (2) and (3) - Legal Protection:

Par. (2) The Privilege of the Writ of Habeas Corpus shall not be suspended, unless when in Cases of Rebellion or Invasion the public Safety may require it.

Par. (3) No Bill of Attainder or ex post facto Law shall be passed.

Article III, Sec. 2, Par. (3) - Trial of All Crimes:

The Trial of all Crimes, except in Cases of Impeachment, shall be by Jury; and such Trial shall be held in the State where the said Crimes shall have been committed; but when not committed within any State, the Trial shall be at such Place or Places as the Congress may by Law have directed.

Article IV, Sec. 2, Par. (1) - Privileges and Immunities:

The Citizens of each State shall be entitled to all Privileges and Immunities of Citizens in the several States.

RIGHTS OF THE PEOPLE - CONSTITUTIONAL AMENDMENTS

Article V - The Amendment Process:

The Congress, whenever two thirds of both Houses shall deem it necessary, shall propose Amendments to this Constitution, or, on the Application of the Legislatures of two thirds of the several States, shall call a Convention for proposing Amendments, which, in either Case, shall be valid to all Intents and Purposes, as Part of this Constitution, when ratified by the Legislatures of three fourths of the several States, or by Conventions in three fourths thereof, as the one or the other Mode of Ratification may be proposed by the Congress; Provided that no Amendment which may be made prior to the Year One thousand eight hundred and eight shall in any Manner affect the first and fourth Clauses in the Ninth Section of the first Article; and that no State, without its Consent, shall be deprived of its equal Suffrage in the Senate.

The Constitution offers two ways to propose amendments:

1. by the agreement of 2/3rds of both Houses of Congress, or
2. by application of the legislatures of 2/3rds of the states calling a convention.

Either method would be valid if ratified by:

1. the legislatures of 3/4ths of the states, or
2. the conventions in 3/4ths of the states, whichever Congress proposes.

To date Congress has proposed all amendments and only one, the 21st Amendment that repealed prohibition, has been ratified by state conventions.

Concerning "the Year One thousand eight hundred and eight," which refers to the importation of slaves, Congress in 1808 banned the African slave trade.

The 104th Congress and the Amendment Process

The Founding Fathers, by intent, made it difficult to pass an amendment to the Constitution. They understood that there are times in history when the majority is wrong and the minority is right about an important national issue. For this reason they structured two houses of Congress which, even in ordinary times, are quite different. This difference became magnified in the 104th Congress.

Congressional Composition before and after the November, 1994 midterm election:

Congressional Composition

1993-94		1995-96	
103rd Congress		*104th Congress*	
House:	258 D	House:	204 D
	176 R		230 R
	1 Ind		1 Ind.
Senate:	56 D	Senate:	46 D
	44 R		54 R
(Counting Sen. Richard Shelby, Sen. Ben Nighthorse Campbell and Representative Nathan Deal as Democrats)		(Counting Sen. Richard Shelby, Sen. Ben Nighthorse Campbell and Representative Nathan Deal as Republicans)	

The mid-term November, 9, 1994 election shifted congressional power from the Democrats to the Republicans. This change was the most dramatic for the House of Representatives. That body, under the leadership of House Speaker Newt Gingrich, immediately launched a fast moving, cohesive Republican agenda. The first phase of their 100 day "Contract with America" was rolling non-stop until they presented the more deliberate Senate with a balanced budget amendment at the end of February, 1995.

In the Senate there was more serious opposition to this amendment. After much debate the voting took place on March 3rd. When it was determined that the amendment was going to be defeated by one vote (a single Republican holdout), majority leader Bob Dole, resorting to a Senate parliamentary maneuver, changed his vote from a yes to a no. The amendment was set aside allowing it to be given reconsideration at a later date.

First attempts in the House to draft an amendment limiting congressional terms met with less than solid Republican support. The final vote taken on March 30th fell far short of the necessary 290 votes (2/3rds of the total House membership) required to pass the amendment.

At this time the Supreme Court had on its 1995 agenda a case concerning term limits which it was expected to act on before summer. The Court's decision would determine whether or not it is constitutional for the state involved to impose restrictions on congressional term limits. This decision would not prevent Congress from reintroducing a term limit amendment, but could influence public opinion around the country. (See *The Way of Politics and Elections in America* - the Supreme Court and term limits.)

The Bill of Rights

Thomas Jefferson, James Madison and others felt that the Constitution had not gone far enough to protect U.S. citizens from the encroachment of federal power. As a result, two years after the Constitution had been signed consideration was being given to its amendment.

In 1789 Congress submitted 12 amendments to the states for ratification signed by:

The Clerk of the House of Representatives
Speaker of the House
Thomas Jefferson, Secretary of State
John Adams, Vice President and President of the Senate

Only 10 of the proposed amendments, identified as the Bill of Rights, were ratified and became a part of the Constitution on December 15, 1791. It would remain for the **14th Amendment** (1868) to requre that parts of the Bill of Rights apply to the states as well as to the federal government.

1st Amendment - Our Freedoms

"Congress shall make no law" concerning the establishment of religion or the prohibition of its free exercise. There shall also be no law obstructing freedom of speech or the press; or the right of people to peaceably assemble or petition the government for help concerning their grievances.

This more than any other article of the Constitution defines the American character. However, many people today wonder if the nation is mature enough to cope with the **1st Amendment**. It does not promise unlimited freedom. Each person's freedoms must of necessity be modified so that others have a chance to express the same freedoms. The success of the 1st amendment lies not in the law, but in the hearts of the people under the law.

2nd Amendment - Right (of the Militia) to Bear Arms

Well regulated Militias are deemed necessary for the security of the free states and their right to bear arms is not to be infringed upon.

The **2nd Amendment** was intended to prevent Congress from being able to disarm the state Militias. It does not apply to the states or private ownership of firearms for reasons other than the state Militias.

According to a Children's Defense Fund report released January 20, 1994, guns in the United States at that time were taking the life of a child every two hours. The Supreme Court has consistently upheld the rights of states to regulate firearms in the interest of public safety.

3rd Amendment - Quartering of Troops

Soldiers in time of peace are not to be quartered in private homes without the owners' consent; nor in time of war, unless prescribed by law.

All during the French and Indian wars the colonies had to put up with British troops on their door steps. It was an experience they were not willing to repeat. The **3rd Amendment** became one of our foundations of the right to privacy- a right that seems to be losing ground in the modern world.

4th Amendment - Search and Seizure

"The right of the people to be secure in their persons, houses, papers, and effects, against unreasonable searches and seizures, shall not be violated." No warrants will be issued except "upon probable cause, supported by Oath or affirmation," describing in particular the place that is to be searched and the persons or things to be seized.

The **4th Amendment** has been made a part of the due process clause and applies to local state and federal law enforcement officers, but not individuals operating on their own.

The key word in this amendment is "unreasonable." It can refer to items searched for or seized or the fact that the search itself is unreasonable. Warrants usually furnish law enforcement officers with adequate protection against any accusation that the **4th Amendment** has been violated, and there are some legal exceptions to the warrant in cases of search and seizure. However, this amendment has had a profound affect on police procedure.

5th Amendment - Protection from Government Authority

1. No person will be held to answer for a capital crime without the presentment or indictment of a grand jury (the military excepted).
2. Whether a person is found to be innocent or guilty in court, the clause related to double jeopardy protects the person against being prosecuted or punished again for the same offense.
3. One cannot be forced to be a witness against one's self, "nor be deprived of life, liberty, or property, without due process of law."

4. Private property cannot be taken by the federal government for public use without just compensation.

The Supreme Court, in interpreting the **14th Amendment**, has decided indictment by grand jury does not come under due process in the case of state trials. The rest of the **5th Amendment** does.

The grand jury, one of the oldest legal safeguards in British law, accepts evidence which it collects for itself or obtains from the legal prosecuting officer in the case. Some states no longer require grand juries or only resort to them when a life sentence or the death sentence might be involved.

If a grand jury is not used, arresting charges are presented by the prosecution in an affidavit, which is a written statement sworn on oath to be true. When the accused is being held in custody, there will also be a hearing held before a magistrate.

6th Amendment - Criminal Court Procedures

The accused shall:

1. have the right to a speedy, public trial, by an impartial jury, in the state and district where the crime is committed;
2. be informed of the nature and cause of the accusation;
3. have the right to see witnesses face to face who are testifying for the prosecution;
4. have a mandatory process of obtaining witnesses for the defense;
5. have counsel for the defense.

Anyone is entitled to a jury trial who demands it,but in a misdemeanor court only a six-person jury is required. Prostitution, petty thieving and drunkenness are the kinds of behaviors brought before this court.

All of the 6th Amendment comes under due process and must be taken into account in both federal and state criminal trials. The right to a speedy and public trial could be a very important factor. If extreme delay is not reasonably accounted for the charges could be dropped.

In this country since the burden of proof does not lie with the defense as the accused is presumed to be innocent, it is the prosecution that must prove to the jury that the accused is guilty.

7th Amendment - Common Law Upheld

"In Suits at common law, where the value in controversy shall exceed twenty dollars, the right of trial by jury shall be preserved." No fact tried by a jury is to be re-examined in any court of the United States except according to the rules of common law.

The **7th Amendment** refers to federal civil suits only. A jury is to be provided if requested. A six-person jury is considered adequate.

8th Amendment - Excessive Bail and Punishment Concerning Criminal Cases

"Excessive bail shall not be required, nor excessive fines imposed, nor cruel and unusual punishment inflicted."

The **8th Amendment** is not part of due process, but must be considered in the sentencing for a capital crime.

At the time the **8th Amendment** was ratified cruel punishment did exist. In this and other countries people were burned at the stake, and many torture devices were still in use throughout the world as means of punishment or to extract information.

The Bill of Rights in its entirety made a tremendous contribution toward humane government.

9th Amendment - Rights of the People

"The enumeration in the Constitution, of certain rights, shall not be construed to deny or disparage others retained by the people."

10th Amendment - Powers of the States and the People

"The powers not delegated to the United States by the Constitution, nor prohibited by it to the States, are reserved to the States respectively, or to the people."

The **9th and 10th Amendments** make it clear that although the federal government must function within the framework of what is stated in the Constitution, the states and more importantly, the people, have powers and rights beyond those specifically granted or denied them in the Constitution.

Post Civil War 13th and 14th Amendments

The most tragic experience the country has ever had to face ultimately shaped us into a nation more in line with our basic philosophy of government.

The **13th Amendment**, proposed on January 31, 1865 and ratified on December 6, 1865, abolished slavery. The **14th Amendment**, proposed on June 13, 1866 and ratified on July 9, 1868, made the privileges of citizenship a reality for all former slaves. This amendment's extension of much of the Bill of Rights beyond the federal government to the states reduced the power of the states over the people.

African-Americans still had a long way to go, but the **13th and 14th Amendments** gave them an imperative beginning. It brought them under the Constitution.

Constitutional References

13th Amendment - The Abolition of Slavery:

> **Section 1.** Neither slavery nor involuntary servitude, except as a punishment for crime whereof the party shall have been duly convicted, shall exist within the United States, or any place subject to their jurisdiction.
>
> **Section 2.** Congress shall have the power to enforce this article by appropriate legislation.

Congress was not only granted power over the question of slavery in Section 2, but also, in time, over the whole subject of racial discrimination extending beyond African-Americans.

14th Amendment, Sec. 1 - Citizenship:

> **Section 1.** All persons born or naturalized in the United States, and subject to the jurisdiction thereof, are citizens of the United States and of the State wherein they reside. No State shall make or enforce any law which shall abridge the privileges or immunities of citizens of the United States; nor shall any State deprive any person of life, liberty, or property, without due process of law; nor deny to any person within its jurisdiction the equal protection of the laws.

Today U.S. citizenship can come about automatically by birth, blood relation or by naturalization through an act of Congress. All native Americans, including the most native of all, American Indians, are now citizens of the United States. Congress can confer citizenship, but the Supreme Court does not allow Congress the privilege of taking away citizenship except in special cases.

The **13th Amendment** replaced parts of two articles in the body of the Constitution: **Article I, Sec. 9, Par. (1)** - the importation of slaves; and **Article IV, Sec. 2, Par. (3)** - the fugitive slave law.

The **14th Amendment, Sec. 2**, changed representation in the House of Representatives as originally designated in **Article I, Sec. 2, Par. (3)**. As it turned out, this change gave the former slave states more representation than they had before the war. The **14th Amendment** said that representation would be reduced in any state that interfered with an eligible person's right to vote in state or national elections, but Congress has never acted on that clause.

Article I, Sec. 2, Par. (3)

Original State Representation in the House of Representatives
Representatives and direct Taxes shall be apportioned among the several States which may be included within this Union, according to their respective Numbers, which shall be determined by adding to the whole Number of free Persons, including those bound to Service for a Term of Years, and excluding Indians not taxed, three fifths of all other Persons.

People "bound to Service for a Term of Years" were indentured servants; "three fifths of all other Persons" were slaves who, after much debate, had been partially counted in representation for the slave states. The 14th Amendment makes no reference to either group.

14th Amendment, Sec. 2
Replaces Article I, Sec. 2, Par. (3)

Section 2. Representatives shall be apportioned among the several States according to their respective numbers, counting the whole number of persons in each State, excluding Indians not taxed.

Voting Rights

83 years after the Constitution was written --- the **15th Amendment** gave male African-Americans, 21 years or older, the right to vote.

133 years after the Constitution was written --- the **19th Amendment** gave all females age 21 or older the right to vote.

177 years after the Constitution was written --- the **24th Amendment** prohibited any state from having a poll tax or any other tax designed to discourage anyone from voting in national elections.

184 years after the Constitution was written --- the **26th Amendment** lowered the voting age to 18 years old.

Law and Order

Constitutional Reference

Article IV, Sec. 2, Par. (2) - Extradition:

> A Person charged in any State with Treason, Felony, or other Crime, who shall flee from Justice, and be found in another State, shall on Demand of the executive Authority of the State from which he fled, be delivered up, to be removed to the State having Jurisdiction of the Crime.

If the crime is not committed in a state, Congress will determine the place of trial as in treason.

This extradition law also extends to other countries. Some countries have proved to be more cooperative than others, but wherever the United States has a reciprocal agreement and exercises its right to request the return of a fugitive, the request should be granted.

Miranda v Arizona (1966) - The Supreme Court and Police Procedure

The Supreme Court is not rigid about what elements make up due process, preferring to draw conclusions from a case as a whole. However, after observing the civil rights breakdown in the area of arrest and police interrogation, when it got to *Miranda,* the court decided to establish some definite rules of procedure. No conviction can now stand unless the following steps have been taken:

1. The accused must be notified of their right to remain silent after arrest and the fact that what they say can be used against them in court.
2. They must be told that their attorneys can be present during questioning and one will be provided for them if they don't have one of their own or cannot afford one.

3. And they must be made aware of the fact that they can terminate an interrogation at any time.

Capital Crimes

1st Degree Murder - premeditated, planned in advance

2nd Degree Murder - not planned in advance

1st Degree Manslaughter - intent to injure only

2nd Degree Manslaughter - the result of reckless action with no intent to injure or kill

Criminally Negligent Manslaughter - complete lack of realization that one's actions could lead to injury or death

These crimes, not mentioned specifically in the Constitution, are upheld among the states with charges and penalties varying from state to state. The degree of criminality is based on a person's *intent* to harm or kill, not on the *result* of harm to or death of the victim. Something to keep in mind if you are ever on a jury.

Trial by Jury

Article III, Sec. 2, Par. (3) in the body of the Constitution guarantees a jury trial for all federal crimes. This was reinforced by the **6th Amendment,** which in turn was extended to the states by the **14th Amendment, Sec. 1.**

It was originally presumed under British common law that there should be 12 persons on a jury with a unanimous verdict in relation to dealing with serious crimes. Then the Supreme Court in 1970 decided that the number 12 is not a vital part of the **6th Amendment.**

Verdicts still must be unanimous in federal courts and in any court where there is a jury of 6 - the minimum number required by law. Beyond this point state legislatures can establish their own rules. However, most of them continue to adhere to the traditional pattern. The Supreme Court has upheld criminal convictions rendered by 9 of a jury of 12 members.

Odds and Ends

Would You Like to Have a Title of Nobility?

Article I, Sec. 9, Par. (8) - Concerning the Federal Government:

> No Title of Nobility shall be granted by the United States: And no Person holding any Office of Profit or Trust under them, shall, without the Consent of the Congress, accept of any present, Emolument, Office, of Title, of any kind whatever, from any King, Prince, or foreign State.

Article I, Sec. 10, Par. (1) - Concerning the States:

> No State shall --- grant any Title of Nobility.

The last part of **Article I, Sec. 9, Par. (8)** was a precaution against a foreign state being able to have special influence on any person or agency in the government of the United States.

Americans have been known to buy titles of individuals in other countries, which may enhance them socially, but are of no legal value in this country.

The First Americans

Our Unwritten Rights Under
the United States Constitution:
the right to make mistakes
and correct them;
the right to forgive and forget;
the right to grow and
adjust our laws accordingly.

ORIGINS

Polynesians from the islands of the South Pacific were the ancestors of natives found in the Hawaiian Islands by European explorers. This chapter covers the rest of the states that have Indian ancestry.

Archaeologists disagree on how long human beings have been on this continent, but there is a general consensus in the white world that at the end of the last ice age some crossed the Bering Strait from Siberia to Alaska on a natural land bridge uncovered by the receded waters. As time went on they are believed to have spread out into Canada, the United States and Latin America. In Alaska Russian explorers found Eskimos, their cousins the Aleuts and Indian tribes such as the Tlingit, Haida, Athapaskan (Athabascan) and Tsimshian. Definite evidence places the ancestors of modern Indians on the U.S. mainland between 15,000 and 14,000 years ago.

Numerous works of ancient mound builders can be found in the eastern part of the United States. Two of the most remarkable earth structures are in Ohio and Illinois. In Illinois the earth pyramid called Monk's Mound covers about 16 acres with a base that has a larger circumference than Egypt's Great Pyramid. Ohio's serpentine mound, 1/4th of a mile long, is the most spectacular when viewed from the air. Its age has not been determined, but some estimates place it as far back as 200 generations ago.

Illinois ultimately became the home of the Algonquian who formed the Illinois Confederacy, but almost faced extinction at the hands of their enemy, the Iroquois. In the same period leading Ohio tribes included the Shawnee, Wyandot, Delaware and Miami.

Folsom Points, prehistoric stone spearheads unearthed near Folsom, New Mexico, are dated before the arrival of the Hohokam, Mongollon, and the Anasazi cliff dwellers who were ancestors of the Pueblo. In this area the Pueblo, in turn, were followed by Navajo, Apache, and Comanche.

Remains of a mammoth and the weapon apparently used to kill it have surfaced in Arizona. In recent history the Apache and Navajo were found on this land. Arizona Indian history is very similar to that of New Mexico.

Cave writings in Southern Nevada and drawings on an enormous boulder called Newspaper Rock in Utah have given us further insight into our first Americans. In Nevada there is evidence of the Pueblo and Basket Makers. Early U.S. scouts found Ute, Paiute, Shoshone and Gosiute in the Utah area. Navajo were later arrivals.

THE INDIAN/EUROPEAN COLLISION

American Indians were a cross-section of humanity like any large group of people. There were skilled craftsmen, farmers, fishermen, hunters and warriors. Most tribes periodically had to fight to defend their territory. In war some took scalps, made slaves of conquered people, burned villages and torture captives. They considered it part of being a good warrior to see how much could be stolen in raids on enemy camps. Most tribes survived because they understood their world. The intruding Europeans in too many instances were insensitive, domineering, and ruthless in ways the Indians from the outset were unable to understand, adequately adjust to or control.

Indian fighting tactics, in turn, spread great fear among the colonists and caused serious reactions.

At first Indian defeat was a start-stop proposition. There were areas in which Indians and European settlers got along quite well together. But Europeans kept on coming, expanding more and more and increasingly threatening the way of life of the original natives. There seemed to be no end in sight.

When the colonies established the United States of America they also established their dominance in this country. We have always been aggressive about protecting and expanding our concept of democracy. However, in this century Indian sovereignty is making a comeback with the assistance of the very government that over a century ago destroyed it.

Constitutional References

14th Amendment, Sec. 2, 1st sentence
Population Count, House of Representatives
Replaces Article I, Sec. 2, Par. (3)

Representatives shall be apportioned among the several States according to their respective numbers, counting the whole number of persons in each State, excluding Indians not taxed.

Article I, Sec. 8, Par. (3) - Congress and the Commerce Clause

The Congress shall have Power --- To regulate Commerce with foreign Nations, and among the several States, and with the Indian Tribes;

These are the only Constitutional references that specifically refer to American Indians. From this time on all Indian tribal contact was under the jurisdiction of Congress with periodic input from the Supreme Court and some presidents, particularly Andrew Jackson.

Timetable of the Eclipse of the Indian World

1775-1788 Under the Continental Congress and Articles of Confederation the states accepted the principle that Congress should manage trade and Indian affairs. A law was passed indicating that all attempts to obtain Indian land titles had to go through Congress. Involvement with American Indians was put under the jurisdiction of the Secretary of War.

1789 In accordance with **Article I, Sec. 8, Par. (3)** of the Constitution, in four statutes Congress established federal authority to make war, govern territories, establish treaties and authorize money to deal with American Indians. At this time contact with Indians in the West had hardly begun and settlements with all Indians was by treaty.

1803 After the Louisiana Purchase that opened up such an enormous track of land in the West, President Thomas Jefferson introduced the idea of moving all Indian tribes west of the Mississippi River for the safety of both the Indians and white settlers. Settlers had become so afraid of Indian fighting tactics that they stayed ready to shoot any Indian who made the slightest move that could be interpreted as confrontational.

1819 Congress created a special fund for the "civilization of the Indians."

1824 The Secretary of War established the Bureau of Indian Affairs.

1830 The Indian Removal Act was passed by Congress.

1831 The Supreme Court, *Cherokee Nation v Georgia*: the Court reviewed protests of the Cherokee concerning their pending removal by the state of Georgia under the Indian Removal Act to Oklahoma territory. Chief Justice Marshall, speaking for the court said" --- the several Indian nations as distinct political communities, having territorial boundaries, within which their authority is exclusive --- is not only acknowledged but guaranteed by the United States."

But it wasn't.

1832 - 1842 President Andrew Jackson ignored the Supreme Court and ordered relocation of the Five Civilized Tribes in the southeast, even though at one point in his career his life had been saved by a Cherokee Indian. Large numbers of Cherokee, Chickasaw, Seminole, Chocktaw and Creek were marched under military guard to the territory of Oklahoma. Thousands died along this *Trail of Tears*.

1849 Congress transferred the Bureau of Indian Affairs from the War Department to the newly established Department of the Interior. An era began in which land, as territory opened up in the West, was set aside for Indian reservations.

1866 Once again Congress declared a treaty null and void and established a new one that better suited it's purpose. The Five Civilized Tribes were required to give up the western half of their new lands to accommodate 20 tribes from Kansas and Nebraska being placed on 13 reservations in the Oklahoma territory. In this period the handling of American Indians resembled a western cattle drive.

1867-1868 The Indian Peace Commission signed 370 treaties with Indian tribes, the last being with the Nez Percé, in August, 1868. Since then, beginning in 1871, all agreements made with Indian groups or individual Indians have been by acts of Congress and executive (presidential) orders or agreements.

1869 Completion of the first transcontinental railroad linking the East and West in 1869 meant faster and better communication for America, but nearly caused the extinction of Indians in the West. Buffalo could not be taught to stay off of railroad tracks and herds of them were known to placidly stand on tracks blocking the advancement of trains. This resulted in government supervision of an all-out campaign to eliminate them. American hide hunters were eager to comply. The mission was virtually accomplished, but because the western Indians were dependent on buffalo for food, clothing, housing, and many survival tools, they also perished in large numbers.

Seeing the Light

1901 When everybody got a change to settle down and people were no longer motivated by fear, American Indians began to receive needed attention. In 1901 citizenship was granted to Indians in designated territories.

1907 Supreme Court, *Winters v United States*: The right of the U.S. Government to reserve waters for the use of Indian tribes was upheld.

1924 All Indians born within the territorial limits of the United States became U.S. citizens. Total citizenship came in part as a result of the remarkable number of Indians who fought with the United States in WWI. They have been in every war in which this nation has been involved since that time, some winning the highest awards the country can give.

1933 Steps were taken to give Indians the right to practice their own customs and religion.

1934 The Indian Reorganization Act was designed to move Indians toward self-sufficiency and self-government through councils elected by the adults of the tribe. This was the beginning of a policy to phase out the Bureau of Indian Affairs.

1944 The first all-Indian political organization in the United States, the National Congress of American Indians, was organized in Denver, Colorado.

1946 Approval of Congress to file claims against the government was no longer required. By congressional act an Indian Claims Commission was established to hear all Indian tribal claims.

1948 Statement of the Hoover Commission concerning American Indians: "Assimilation must be the dominant goal."

1951 The Bureau of Indian Affairs objective: "A standard of living for Indians comparable with that enjoyed by other elements of our society."

1968 The Civil Rights Act guaranteed certain rights to Indians under tribal governments and repealed the 1953 act allowing states extended jurisdiction in tribal affairs without tribal consent.

1969 The Ninth Circuit Court of Appeals upheld a freeze on the acquisition of land in Alaska and enforced native rights and use of the land in question.

1980 Supreme Court, *United States v Sioux Nation of Indians*: the federal government was ordered to pay approximately $105 million to eight Sioux Indian tribes for land in South Dakota seized by the United States in 1877.

TODAY

Who is Indian

The U.S. Census Bureau accepts anyone as Indian who says he or she is Indian. Tribes vary on the amount of Indian blood they feel a person must have to become a member of their particular tribe.

In the face of these variables the 1990 Census indicated there were 1,878,285 American Indians in the country. In 1987 the Bureau of Indian Affairs had estimated 861,000 were living on or adjacent to reservations. Alaska's native Indians, Eskimos and Aleuts numbered 85,698 in 1990, with Eskimos representing more than half of that population.

Defining a Tribe

Originally the definition of a tribe meant the grouping of a body of people who had blood ties and like views and practices concerning their language, religion, customs and methods of governing themselves. This definition became blurred with the advancement of settlers and constant displacement of tribes by the federal government.

War between the state of Florida and remnant Indian bands waged from 1835 to 1842 virtually destroyed the Seminole left in that area. The Sauk and Fox, who eventually combined to strengthen their ranks, were moved from Michigan to Wisconsin, then Iowa and Kansas before being finally allowed to settle in Oklahoma. The Shawnee, Delaware, Kickapoo and Winnebago, like the Sauk and Fox, were moved so frequently that they never had a chance to adjust to new and totally different environments. They died in large numbers of disease and starvation.

It is estimated that at one time there were over 300 different Indian languages. Approximately 250 do still exist. Languages spoken the most are the Cherokee (Iroquoian), Navajo (Athapaskan) and Titon Sioux (Siouan).

Government Trusteeship

The word "reservation" began to be used in the days when the federal government took over Indian lands by treaty reserving a part designated by the Indians for their own use. The Indian right to the return of some of this land is not an act of charity. It is acknowledgment of the fact that Indians have the same rights of inheritance from their ancestors as other American citizens do from theirs.

Whatever non-recurring money is paid by the federal government to Indian tribes or individuals is compensation for Indian losses resulting from treaty violations or government seizure of Indian lands. Tribes or individuals may receive government checks for income from *their* land and its resources, but that is because these assets are being held in trust by the Secretary of the Interior. Payment for the use of these resources has been collected by the federal government.

Government to Government

One of the most remarkable developments is the fact that the Bureau of Indian Affairs now deals with many Indian tribes as individual governments. This has resulted in the United States returning to divided sovereignty among the states, our central government and Indian nations, only this time there is cooperation instead of conflict.

On the Reservation

Indians on or off of reservations are American citizens with the privileges and responsibilities of other citizens. However, reservation Indians are expected to abide by the rules established by their tribe. Most reservations are entirely self-governing.

Each reservation determines who is classified as a tribal member in regard to the amount of Indian blood, whether or not there can be individual land ownership, and whether or not non-Indians can reside on their reservation. They also establish their source and amount of reservation revenue and local voting rights.

Some reservations are very small while others encompass many acres. According to the Bureau of Indian Affairs the Navajo (population about 219 thousand) cover 16 million acres in the states of Utah, Arizona and New Mexico. A total of 53 million acres of land is currently being held in trust by the United States for Indian tribes and individuals. Not all reservation land is trust land.

State law does not apply to Indian reservations, but federal law makes it a federal offense to violate a state's criminal laws on any reservation.

In the area of taxes, Indians are exempt from paying federal taxes on income derived from land held in trust by the United Sates. They also are exempt from paying local property tax on reservation or trust lands. They do pay state sales tax on any purchases made off of their reservation, and state income tax if they are employed in a state instead of on their reservation.

RETURN OF THE CHEROKEE

The body of the Cherokee Nation, originally the largest tribe in the southeast, still resides in Oklahoma, but some returned to their homeland, the Great Smoky Mountains of Western North Carolina. Here a flame burns continuously as a symbol of the epic restoration. The flame is at the entrance of an outdoor theater with tiered seats hugging the mountainside. This is where "Unto These Hills," the drama of the Cherokee exodus to Oklahoma, is performed. People from all over the country come to see it.

This writer, who currently lives in the Smokies within an hour's drive along the Blue Ridge Parkway of this Cherokee federal reservation, interviewed the Chief and Superintendent of the Bureau of Indian Affairs in August, 1993.

Jonathan L. Taylor, Chief of the Cherokee Tribal Council, was elected by the people and functions in a legislative as well as executive capacity. He fills both the role of a governor and lobbyist in Washington on behalf of his tribe.

Chief Taylor had a Cherokee father and white mother, and like his father, married a white woman. His children, 1/4th Cherokee, will inherit his considerable private land holdings, but he says that his wife cannot inherit.

Cherokee Superintendent of the Bureau of Indian Affairs, Wilbur Paul, owns land in the west which some of his relatives occupy, but he prefers living in the Great Smokies.

The Cherokee run their entire reservation including their school. Although there is no tax on land, there is a reservation levy and federal tax. One of their main sources of revenue is tourism. This is the most traveled national park area in the country.

The Cherokee are no longer spread across West Virginia, Virginia, North and South Carolina, Kentucky, Tennessee, Georgia and Alabama. However in the 1990 census, numbering 308 thousand, they became the largest tribe in the country.

OKLAHOMA

Oklahoma is one of our finest examples of Indian/settler blending that survived very adverse conditions.

After the Five Civilized Tribes, between 1832 and 1842, were driven to Oklahoma territory 20 more tribes were brought in from the East. In 1889 the government again carved up the region to give white settlers two million acres, and there were more to come. Arapaho, Caddo, Kiowa, Wichita, Osage, Pawnee, Cheyenne and Comanche were already in this territory when these migrations began.

Today approximately 1/8th of the nation's Indian population resides in Oklahoma where almost 70 tribes are represented. There are no formal reservations in this state.

American Indians have helped form the Oklahoma state Constitution, been in the state legislature and Supreme Court, U.S. Senate, and have held the offices of governor and Vice President of the United States. (See Charles Curtis - Election of '92.) Will Rogers, part Cherokee and proud of it, was embraced by all of America as a writer, actor and humorist. Jim Thorpe, of Sauk and Fox heritage, was called by the King of Sweden the greatest athlete in the world. In the 1912 World Olympics Thorpe was the first man in history to win both the pentathlon and decathlon gold medals. He was also admitted to the Football Hall of Fame in 1951. Oklahoma celebrates Will Rogers day every November 4th, and in Pennsylvania a town is called Jim Thorpe.

Final Note

In October, 1993, a tall grass reserve was established in Oklahoma so that the buffalo could run free again in that part of the West.

Are We a Republic or a Democracy?

The Constitution never mentions the word democracy, but does guarantee every state a republican form of government **(Article IV, Sec. 4).**

Both forms of government are for the people with representatives elected by the people. Yet some countries of the world that call themselves republics are really functioning as dictatorships.

Our Constitution has provided for all of the people to participate in choosing representatives at every level - from the small Alaskan town of North Pole to our national seat of government in Washington, DC.

In this country We are the government, and, America, you can't get any more *democratic* than that!

Part IV

Our Constitution

Constitutional Changes

1. **Article I, Sec. 2, Par. (3)**
   First sentence replaced by the *14th Amendment, Sec. 2*

2. **Article I, Sec. 3, Par. (1)**
   Replaced by the *17th Amendment, Par.(1)*

3. **Article I, Sec. 3, Par. (2)**
   Modified by the *17th Amendment, Par.(2)*

4. **Article I, Sec. 2, Par. (4)**
   Modified by the *17th Amendment, Par.(2)*

5. **Article I, Sec. 4, Par. (1)**
   Modified by the *17th Amendment*

6. **Article I, Sec. 4, Par. (2)**
   Replaced by the *20th Amendment, Sec. 1 and 2*

7. **Article I, Sec. 9, Par. (1)**
   Canceled by the *13th Amendment*

8. **Article I, Sec. 9, Par. (4)**
   Canceled by the *16th Amendment*

9. **Article I, Sec. 10, Par. (1)**
   Modified: letters of marque and reprisal outlawed

10. **Article II, Sec. 1, Par. (1)**
    Extended by the *22th Amendment*

11. **Article II, Sec. 1, Par. (3)**
    Replaced by the *12th Amendment*

12. **Articles II, Sec. 1, Par. (6)**
    Extended by the *20th Amendment, Sec. 3 and 4*
    Further extended by the *25th Amendment*

13. **Article III, Sec. 2, Par. (1)**
    Modified by the *11th Amendment*

14. **Article IV, Sec. 2, Par. (3)**
    Canceled by the *13th Amendment*

15. **1st, 4th, 5th and 6th Amendments**
    Federal "due process" and "equal protection" extended in part to the states by the *14th Amendment, Sec. 1*

16. **18th Amendment**
    Repealed by the *21st Amendment*

17. **24th Amendment**
    Unnecessary. The Supreme Court decided in *Harper v Virginia Board of Education* (1966) that the equal protection clause of the *14th Amendment, Sec. 1* adequately covers discrimination against voters at the polls.

The Constitution of the United States of America

(Proposed, 1787; Ratified, 1788)

We the People of the United States, in Order to form a more perfect Union, establish Justice, insure domestic Tranquility, provide for the common defence, promote the general Welfare, and secure the Blessings of Liberty to ourselves and our Posterity, do ordain and establish this Constitution for the United States of America.

ARTICLE I

Section 1. All legislative Powers herein granted shall be vested in a Congress of the United Sates, which shall consist of a Senate and House of Representatives.

Section 2. Par. (1) The House of Representatives shall be composed of Members chosen every second Year by the People of the several States, and the Electors in each State shall have the Qualifications requisite for Electors of the most numerous Branch of the State Legislature.

Par. (2) No Person shall be a Representative who shall not have attained to the Age of twenty five Years, and been seven Years a Citizen of the United States, and who shall not, when elected, be an Inhabitant of that State in which he shall be chosen.

Par. (3) Representatives and direct Taxes shall be apportioned among the several States which may be included within this Union, according to their respective Numbers, which shall be determined by adding to the whole Number of free Persons, including those bound to Service for a Term of Years, and excluding Indians not taxed, three fifths of all other Persons. The actual Enumeration shall be made within three Years after the first Meeting of the Congress of the United States, and within every subsequent Term of ten Years, in such Manner as they shall by Law direct. The Number of Representatives shall not exceed one for every thirty Thousand, but each State shall have at Least one Representative; and until such enumerations shall be made, the State of New Hampshire shall be entitled to chuse three, Massachusetts eight, Rhode-Island and Providence Plantations one, Connecticut five, New-York six, New Jersey four, Pennsylvania eight, Delaware one, Maryland six, Virginia ten, North Carolina five, South Carolina five, and Georgia three.

Par. (4) When vacancies happen in the Representation from any State, the Executive Authority thereof shall issue Writs of Election to fill such Vacancies.

Par. (5) The House of Representatives shall chuse their speaker and other Officers; and shall have the sole Power of Impeachment.

Section 3. Par. (1) The Senate of the United States shall be composed of two Senators from each State, chosen by the Legislature thereof, for six Years; and each Senator shall have one Vote.

Par. (2) Immediately after they shall be assembled in Consequence of the first Election, they shall be divided as equally as may be into three Classes. The Seats of the Senators of the first Class shall be vacated at the Expiration of the second Year, of the second Class at the Expiration of the fourth Year, and of the third Class at the Expiration of the sixth Year, so that one third may be chosen every second Year; and if Vacancies happen by Resignation, or otherwise, during the Recess of the Legislature of any State, the Executive thereof may make temporary Appointments until the next Meeting of the Legislature, which shall then fill such Vacancies.

Par. (3) No person shall be a Senator who shall not have attained to the Age of thirty Years, and been nine Years a Citizen of the United States, and who shall not, when elected, be an Inhabitant of that State for which he shall be chosen.

Par. (4) The Vice President of the United States shall be President of the Senate, but shall have no Vote, unless they be equally divided.

Par. (5) The Senate shall choose their other Officers, and also a President pro tempore, in the Absence of the Vice President, or when he shall exercise the Office of President of the United States.

Par. (6) The Senate shall have the sole Power to try all Impeachments. When sitting for that Purpose, they shall be on Oath or Affirmation. When the President of the United States is tried, the Chief Justice shall preside: And no Person shall be convicted without the concurrence of two thirds of the Members present. Judgment in Cases of Impeachment shall not extend further than to removal from Office, and disqualification to hold and enjoy any Office of honor, Trust or Profit under the United States: but the Party convicted shall nevertheless be liable and subject to Indictment, Trial, Judgment and Punishment, according to Law.

Section 4. Par. (1) The Times, Places and Manner of holding Elections for Senators and Representatives, shall be prescribed in each State by the Legislature thereof; but the Congress may at any time by Law make or alter such Regulations, except as to the Places of choosing Senators.

Par. (2) The Congress shall assemble at least once in every Year, and such Meeting shall be on the first Monday in December, unless they shall by Law appoint a different Day.

Section 5. Par. (1) Each House shall be the Judge of the Elections, Returns and Qualifications of its own Members, and a Majority of each shall constitute a Quorum to do Business; but a smaller Number may adjourn from day to day, and may be authorized to compel the Attendance of absent Members, in such Manner, and under such Penalties as each House may provide.

Par. (2) Each House may determine the Rules of its Proceedings, punish its Members for disorderly Behavior, and, with the Concurrence of two thirds, expel a Member.

Par. (3) Each House shall keep a Journal of its Proceedings, and from time to time publish the same, excepting such Parts as may in their Judgment require Secrecy; and the yeas and Nays of the Members of either House on any question shall, at the Desire of one fifth of those Present, be entered on the Journal.

Par. (4) Neither House, during the Session of Congress, shall, without the Consent of the other, adjourn for more than three days, nor to any other Place than that in which the two Houses shall be sitting.

Section 6. Par. (1) The Senators and Representatives shall receive a Compensation for their Services, to be ascertained by Law, and paid out of the Treasury of the United States. They shall in all Cases, except Treason, Felony and Breach of the Peace, be privileged from Arrest during their Attendance at the Session of their respective Houses, and in going to and returning from the same; and for any Speech or Debate in either House, they shall not be questioned in any other Place.

Par. (2) No Senator or Representative shall, during the Time for which he was elected, be appointed to any civil Office under the Authority of the United States, which shall have been created, or the Emoluments whereof shall have been increased during such time; and no Person holding any Office under the United States, shall be a Member of either House during his Continuance in Office.

Section 7. Par. (1) All Bills for raising Revenue shall originate in the House of Representatives; but the Senate may propose or concur with Amendments as on other Bills.

Par. (2) Every Bill which shall have passed the House of Representatives and the Senate, shall, before it become a Law, be presented to the President of the United States; if he approve he shall sign it, but if not he shall return it, with his Objections to that House in which it shall have originated, who shall enter the Objections at large on their Journal, and proceed to reconsider it. If after such Reconsideration two thirds of that House shall agree to pass the Bill, it shall be sent, together with the Objections, to the other House, by which it shall likewise be reconsidered, and if approved by two thirds of that House, it shall become a Law. But in all such Cases the Votes of both Houses shall be determined by yeas and Nays, and the Names of the Persons voting for and against the Bill shall be entered on the Journal of each House respectively. If any Bill shall not be returned by the President within ten days (Sundays excepted) after it shall have been presented to him, the Same shall be a Law, in like Manner as if he had signed it, unless the Congress by their Adjournment prevent its Return, in which Case it shall not be a Law.

Par. (3) Every Order, Resolution, or Vote to which the Concurrence of the Senate and House of Representatives may be necessary (except on a question of Adjournment) shall be presented to the President of the United States; and before the Same shall take Effect, shall be approved by him, or being disapproved by him, shall be repassed by two thirds of the Senate and House of Representatives, according to the Rules and Limitations prescribed in the Case of a Bill.

Section 8. Par. (1) The Congress shall have Power To lay and collect Taxes, Duties, Imposts, and Excises, to pay the Debts and provide for the common Defense and general Welfare of the United States; but all duties, Imposts and Excises shall be uniform throughout the United States.

Par. (2) To borrow Money on the Credit of the United States;

Par. (3) To regulate Commerce with foreign Nations, and among the several States, and with the Indian Tribes;

Par. (4) To establish an uniform Rule of Naturalization, and uniform Laws on the subject of Bankruptcies throughout the United States;

Par. (5) To coin Money, regulate the Value thereof, and of foreign Coin, and fix the Standard of Weights and Measures;

Par. (6) To provide for the Punishment of counterfeiting the Securities and current Coin of the United States;

Par. (7) To establish Post Offices and post Roads;

Par. (8) To promote the Progress of Science and useful Arts, by securing for limited Times to Authors and Inventors the exclusive Right to their respective Writings and Discoveries;

Par. (9) To constitute Tribunals inferior to the supreme Court;

Par. (10) To define and punish Piracies and Felonies committed on the high Seas, and Offenses against the Law of Nations;

Par. (11) To declare War, grant letters of Marque and Reprisal, and make rules concerning Captures on Land and Water;

Par. (12) To raise and support Armies, but no Appropriation of Money to that Use shall be for a longer Term than two Years;

Par. (13) To provide and maintain a Navy;

Par. (14) To make Rules for the Government and Regulation of the land and naval Forces;

Par. (15) To provide for calling forth the Militia to execute the Laws of the Union, suppress Insurrections and repel Invasions;

Par. (16) To provide for organizing, arming, and disciplining, the Militia, and for governing such Part of them as may be employed in the Service of the United States, reserving to the States respectively, the Appointment of the Officers, and the Authority of training the Militia according to the discipline prescribed by Congress;

Par. (17) To exercise exclusive Legislation in all Cases whatsoever, over such District (not exceeding ten Miles square), as may, by Cession of particular States, and the Acceptance of Congress, become the Seat of the Government of the United States, and to exercise like Authority over all Places purchased by the Consent of the Legislature of the State in which the Same shall be for the Erection of Forts, Magazines, Arsenals, dock-Yards, and other needful Buildings; - And

Par. (18) To make all Laws which shall be necessary and proper for carrying into Execution the foregoing Powers, and all other Powers vested by this Constitution in the Government of the United States, or in any Department or Officer thereof.

Section 9. (1) The Migration of Importation of such Persons as any of the States now existing shall think proper to admit, shall not be prohibited by the Congress prior to the Year one thousand eight hundred and eight, but a Tax or duty may be imposed on such Importation, not exceeding ten dollars for each Person.

Par. (2) The Privilege of the Writ of Habeas Corpus shall not be suspended, unless when in Cases of Rebellion or Invasion the public Safety may require it.

Par. (3) No Bill of Attainder or ex post facto Law shall be passed.

Par. (4) No Capitation, or other direct, Tax shall be laid, unless in Proportion to the Census or Enumeration herein before directed to be taken.

Par. (5) No Tax or Duty shall be laid on Articles exported from any State.

Par. (6) No Preference shall be given by any Regulation of Commerce or Revenue to the Ports of one State over those of another: nor shall Vessels bound to, or from, one State, be obliged to enter, clear, or pay Duties in another.

Par. (7) No Money shall be drawn from the Treasury, but in Consequence of Appropriations made by Law; and a regular Statement and Account of the Receipts and Expenditures of all public Money shall be published from time to time.

Par. (8) No Title of Nobility shall be granted by the United States: And no Person holding any Office of Profit or Trust under them, shall, without the Consent of the Congress, accept of any present, Emolument, Office, or Title, of any kind whatever, from any King, Prince, or foreign State.

Section 10. Par. (1) No State shall enter into any Treaty, Alliance, or Confederation; grant Letters of Marque and Reprisal; coin Money; emit Bills of Credit; make any Thing but gold and silver Coin a Tender in Payment of Debts; pass any Bill of Attainder, ex post facto Law, or Law impairing the Obligation of Contracts, or grant any Title of Nobility.

Par. (2) No State shall, without the Consent of the Congress, lay any Imposts or Duties on Imports or Exports, except what may be absolutely necessary for executing its inspection Laws: and the net Produce of all Duties and Imposts, laid by any State on Imports or Exports, shall be for the Use of the Treasury of the United States; and all such Laws shall be subject to the Revision and Controul of the Congress.

Par. (3) No State shall, without the Consent of Congress, lay any Duty of Tonnage, keep Troops, or Ships of War in time of Peace, enter into any Agreement or Compact with another State, or with a foreign Power, or engage in War, unless actually invaded, or in such imminent Danger as will not admit of delay.

ARTICLE II

Section 1. Par. (1) The executive Power shall be vested in a President of the United States of America. He shall hold his Office during the Term of four Years, and, together with the Vice President, chosen for the same Term, be elected, as follows

Par. (2) Each State shall appoint, in such Manner as the Legislature thereof may direct, a Number of Electors, equal to the whole Number of Senators and Representatives to which the State may be entitled in the Congress: but no Senator or Representative, or Person holding an Office of Trust or Profit under the United States, shall be appointed an Elector.

Par. (3) The Electors shall meet in their respective States, and vote by Ballot for two Persons, of who one at least shall not be an Inhabitant of the same State with themselves. And they shall make a List of all the Persons voted for, and of the Number of Votes for each; which List they shall sign and certify, and transmit sealed to the Seat of the Government of the United States, directed to the President of the Senate. The President of the Senate shall, in the Presence of the Senate and House of Representatives, open all the Certificates, and the Votes shall then be counted. The Person having the greatest Number of Votes shall be the President, if such Number be a Majority of the whole Number of Electors appointed; and if there be more than one who have such Majority, and have an equal Number of Votes, then the House of Representatives shall immediately chuse by Ballot one of them for President; and if no Person have a Majority, then from the five highest on the List the said House shall in like Manner chuse the President. But in chusing the President, the Votes shall be taken by States, the Representation from each State having one Vote; A quorum for this

Purpose shall consist of a Member or Members from two thirds of the States, and a Majority of all the States shall be necessary to a Choice. In every Case, after the Choice of the President, the Person having the greatest Number of Votes of the Electors shall be the Vice President. But if there should remain two or more who have equal Votes, the Senate shall chuse from them by Ballot the Vice President.

Par. (4) The Congress may determine the Time of chusing the Electors, and the Day on which they shall give their Votes; which Day shall be the same throughout the United States.

Par. (5) No Person except a natural born Citizen, or a Citizen of the United States, at the time of the Adoption of this Constitution, shall be eligible to the Office of President; neither shall any Person be eligible to that Office who shall not have attained to the Age of thirty five Years, and been fourteen Years a Resident within the United States.

Par. (6) In Case of the Removal of the President from Office, or of his Death, Resignation, or Inability to discharge the Powers and Duties of the said Office, the Same shall devolve on the Vice President, and the Congress may be Law provide for the Case of Removal, Death, Resignation or Inability, both of the President and Vice President, declaring what Officer shall then act as President, and such Officer shall act accordingly, until the Disability be removed, or a President shall be elected.

Par. (7) The President shall, at stated Times, receive for his Services, a Compensation, which shall neither be encreased nor diminished during the Period for which he shall have been elected, and he shall not receive within that Period any other Emolument from the United States, or any of them.

Par. (8) Before he enter on the Execution of his Office, he shall take the following Oath or Affirmation: - "I do solemnly swear (or affirm) that I will faithfully execute the Office of President of the United States, and will to the best of my Ability, preserve, protect and defend the Constitution of the United States."

Section 2. Par. (1) The President shall be Commander in Chief of the Army and Navy of the United States, and of the Militia of the several

States, when called into the actual Service of the United States; he may require the Opinion, in writing, of the principal Officer in each of the executive Departments, upon any Subject relating to the Duties of their respective Offices, and he shall have Power to grant Reprieves and Pardons for Offenses against the United States, except in Cases of Impeachment.

Par. (2) He shall have Power, by and with the Advice and Consent of the Senate, to make Treaties, provided two thirds of the Senators present concur; and he shall nominate, and by and with the Advice and Consent of the Senate, shall appoint Ambassadors, other public Ministers and Consuls, Judges of the supreme Court, and all other Officers of the United States, whose Appointments are not herein otherwise provided for, and which shall be established by Law: but the Congress may by Law vest the Appointment of such inferior Officers, as they think proper, in the President alone, in the Courts of Law, or in the Heads of Departments.

Par. (3) The President shall have Power to fill up all Vacancies that may happen during the Recess of the Senate, by granting Commissions which shall expire at the End of their next Session.

Section 3. He shall from time to time give to the Congress Information of the State of the Union, and recommend to their Consideration such Measures as he shall judge necessary and expedient; he may, on extraordinary Occasions, convene both Houses, or either of them, and in Case of Disagreement between them, with Respect to the Time of Adjournment, he may adjourn them to such Time as he shall think proper; he shall receive Ambassadors and other public Ministers; he shall take Care that the Laws be faithfully executed, and shall Commission all the Officers of the United States.

Section 4. The President, Vice President and all civil Officers of the United States, shall be removed from Office on Impeachment for, and Conviction of, Treason, Bribery, or other High Crimes and Misdemeanors.

ARTICLE III

Section 1. The judicial Power of the United States, shall be vested in one supreme Court, and in such inferior Courts as the Congress may from time to time ordain and establish. The Judges, both of the supreme and inferior Courts, shall hold their Offices during good Behaviour, and shall, at stated Times, receive for their Services, a Compensation, which shall not be diminished during their Continuance in Office.

Section 2. Par. (1) The judicial Power shall extend to all Cases, in Law and Equity, arising under this Constitution, the Laws of the United States, and Treaties made, or which shall be made, under their Authority; - to all Cases affecting Ambassadors, other public Ministers and Consuls; - to all Cases of admiralty and maritime Jurisdiction; - to Controversies to which the United States shall be a Party; - to Controversies between two or more States; between a State and Citizens of another State; - between Citizens of different States; - between Citizens of the same State claiming Lands under Grants of different States, and between a State, or the Citizens thereof, and foreign States, Citizens or Subjects.

Par. (2) In all Cases affecting Ambassadors, other public Ministers and Consuls, and those in which a State shall be Party, the supreme Court shall have original Jurisdiction. In all the other Cases before mentioned, the supreme Court shall have appellate Jurisdiction, both as to Law and Fact, with such Exceptions, and under such Regulations as the Congress shall make.

Par. (3) The Trial of all Crimes, except in Cases of Impeachment, shall be by Jury; and such Trial shall be held in the State where the said Crimes shall have been committed; but when not committed within any State, the Trial shall be at such Place or Places as the Congress may by Law have directed.

Section 3. Par. (1) Treason against the United States, shall consist only in levying War against them, or in adhering to their Enemies, giving them Aid and Comfort. No Person shall be convicted of Treason unless on the

Testimony of two Witnesses to the same overt Act, or on Confession in open Court.

Par. (2) The Congress shall have Power to declare the Punishment of Treason, but no Attainder of Treason shall work Corruption of Blood, or Forfeiture except during the Life of the Person attainted.

Article IV

Section 1. Full Faith and Credit shall be given in each State to the public Acts, Records, and judicial Proceedings of every other State. And the Congress may by general Laws prescribe the Manner in which such Acts, Records and Proceedings shall be proved, and the Effect thereof.

Section 2. Par. (1) The Citizens of each State shall be entitled to all Privileges and Immunities of Citizens in the several States.

Par. (2) A Person charged in any State with Treason, Felony, or other Crime, who shall flee from Justice, and be found in another State, shall on Demand of the executive Authority of the State from which he fled, be delivered up, to be removed to the State having Jurisdiction of the Crime.

Par. (3) No person held to Service or Labour in one State, under the Laws thereof, escaping into another, shall, in Consequence of any Law or Regulation therein, be discharged from such Service or Labour, but shall be delivered up on Claim of the Party to whom such Service or Labour may be due.

Section 3. Par. (1) New States may be admitted by the Congress into this Union; but no new State shall be formed or erected within the Jurisdiction of any other State; nor any State be formed by the Junction of two or more States, or Parts of States, without the Consent of the Legislatures of the States concerned as well as of the Congress.

Par. (2) The Congress shall have Power to dispose of and make all needful Rules and Regulations respecting the Territory or other Property belonging to the United States; and nothing in this Constitution shall be so construed as to Prejudice any Claims of the United States, or of any particular State.

Section 4. The United States shall guarantee to every State in this Union a Republican Form of Government, and shall protect each of them against Invasion; and on Application of the Legislature, or of the Executive (when the Legislature cannot be convened) against domestic Violence.

ARTICLE V

The Congress, whenever two thirds of both Houses shall deem it necessary, shall propose Amendments to this Constitution, or, on the Application of the Legislatures of two thirds of the several States, shall call a Convention for proposing Amendments, which, in either Case, shall be valid to all Intents and Purposes, as Part of this Constitution, when ratified by the Legislatures of three fourths of the several States, or by Conventions in three fourths thereof, as the one or the other Mode of Ratification may be proposed by the Congress; Provided that no Amendment which may be made prior to the Year One thousand eight hundred and eight shall in any Manner affect the first and fourth Clauses in the Ninth Section of the first Article; and that no State, without its Consent, shall be deprived of its equal Suffrage in the Senate.

ARTICLE VI

Par. (1) All Debts contracted and Engagements entered into, before the Adoption of this Constitution, shall be as valid against the United States under this Constitution, as under the Confederation.

Par. (2) This Constitution, and the Laws of the United States which shall be made in Pursuance thereof; and all Treaties made, or which shall be made, under the Authority of the United States, shall be the supreme Law of the Land; and the Judges in every State shall be bound thereby, any Thing in the Constitution or Laws of any State to the Contrary notwithstanding.

Par. (3) The Senators and Representatives before mentioned, and the Members of the several State Legislatures, and all executive and judicial Officers, both of the United States and of the several States, shall be bound by Oath or Affirmation, to support this Constitution; but no religious Test shall ever be required as a Qualification to any Office or public Trust under the United States.

ARTICLE VII

Par. (1) The Ratification of the Conventions of nine States, shall be sufficient for the Establishment of this Constitution between the States so ratifying the Same.

Par. (2) DONE in Convention by the Unanimous Consent of the States present the Seventeenth Day of September in the Year of our Lord one thousand seven hundred and Eighty seven and of the Independence of the United States of America the Twelfth In witness whereof We have hereunto subscribed our Names,

attest William Jackson Secretary

G. Washington- Presidt
and deputy from Virginia

Delaware	Geo: Read Gunning Bedford jun John Dickinson Richard Bassett Jaco: Broom	New Hampshire	John Langdon Nicholas Gilman
		Massachusetts	Nathaniel Gorham Rufus King
Maryland	James McHenry Dan of St Thos Jenifer Danl Carroll	Connecticut	Wm Saml Johnson Roger Sherman
		New York	Alexander Hamilton
Virginia	John Blair___ James Madison Jr.	New Jersey	Will: Livingston David Brearley Wm Paterson Jona: Dayton
North Carolina	Wm Blount Richd Dobbs Spaight Hu Williamson		

South Carolina	J. Rutledge Charles Cotesworth Pinckney Charles Pinckney Pierce Butler	Pennsylvania	B Franklin Thomas Mifflin Robt Morris Geo Clymer Thos FitzSimons Jared Ingersoll James Wilson Gouv Morris
Georgia	William Few Abr Baldwin		

Par. (1) Resolved, that the preceding Constitution be laid before the United States in Congress assembled, and that in the Opinion of this Convention, that it should afterwards be submitted to a Convention of Delegates, chosen in each State by the People thereof, under the Recommendation of its Legislature, for their Assent and Ratification; and that each Convention assenting to, and ratifying the Same, should give Notice thereof to the United States in Congress assembled.

Par. (2) Resolved, That it is the Opinion of this Convention, that as soon as the Conventions of the nine States shall have ratified this Constitution, the United States in Congress assembled should fix a Day on which Electors should be appointed by the States which shall have ratified the same, and a Day on which the Electors should assemble to vote for the President, and the Time and Place for commencing Proceedings under this Constitution. That after such Publication the Electors should be appointed, and the Senators and Representatives elected: That the Electors should meet on the Day fixed for the Election of the President, and should transmit their votes certified signed, sealed and directed, as the Constitution requires, to the Secretary of the United States in Congress assembled, that the Senators and Representatives should convene at the Time and Place assigned; that the Senators should appoint a President of the Senate, for the sole Purpose of receiving, opening and counting the Votes for President; and that after he shall be chosen, the Congress, together with the President, should, without Delay, proceed to execute this Constitution.

By the Unanimous Order of the Convention.

William Jackson
Secretary

G. Washington,
Presidt.

CONSTITUTIONAL AMENDMENTS

ARTICLES IN ADDITION TO, AND AMENDMENT OF THE CONSTITUTION OF THE UNITED STATES OF AMERICA, PROPOSED BY CONGRESS AND RATIFIED BY THE SEVERAL STATES, PURSUANT TO THE FIFTH ARTICLE OF THE ORIGINAL CONSTITUTION.

BILL OF RIGHTS - FIRST 10 AMENDMENTS

(Proposed, 1789; Ratified, 1791)

ARTICLE I = 1st Amendment

Congress shall make no law respecting an establishment of religion, or prohibiting the free exercise thereof; or abridging the freedom of speech, or of the press; or the right of the people peaceably to assemble, and to petition the Government for a redress of grievances.

ARTICLE II = 2nd Amendment

A well regulated Militia, being necessary to the security of a free State, the right of the people to keep and bear Arms, shall not be infringed.

ARTICLE III = 3rd Amendment

No Soldier shall, in time of peace be quartered in any house, without the consent of the Owner, nor in time of war, but in a manner to be prescribed by law.

ARTICLE IV = 4th Amendment

The right of the people to be secure in their persons, houses, papers, and effects, against unreasonable searches and seizures, shall not be violated, and no Warrants shall issue, but upon probable cause, supported by Oath or affirmation, and particularly describing the place to be searched, and the persons or things to be seized.

ARTICLE V = 5th Amendment

No person shall be held to answer for a capital, or otherwise infamous crime, unless on a presentment or indictment of a Grand Jury, except in cases arising in the land or naval forces, or in the Militia, when in actual service in time of War or public danger; nor shall any person be subject for the same offence to be twice put in jeopardy of life or limb; nor shall be compelled in any criminal case to be a witness against himself, nor be deprived of life, liberty, or property, without due process of law; nor shall private property be taken for public use, without just compensation.

ARTICLE VI = 6th Amendment

In all criminal prosecutions, the accused shall enjoy the right to a speedy and public trial, by an impartial jury of the State and district wherein the crime shall have been committed, which district shall have been previously ascertained by law, and to be informed of the nature and cause of the accusation; to be confronted with the witnesses against him; to have compulsory process for obtaining witnesses in his favor, and to have the Assistance of Counsel for his defence.

ARTICLE VII = 7th Amendment

In Suits of common law, where the value in controversy shall exceed twenty dollars, the right of trial by jury shall be preserved, and no fact tried by a jury, shall be otherwise re-examined in any Court of the United States, than according to the rules of the common law.

ARTICLE VIII = 8th Amendment

Excessive bail shall not be required, nor excessive fines imposed, nor cruel and unusual punishments inflicted.

ARTICLE IX = 9th Amendment

The enumeration in the Constitution, of certain rights, shall not be construed to deny or disparage others retained by the people.

ARTICLE X = 10th Amendment

The powers not delegated to the United States by the Constitution, nor prohibited by it to the States, are reserved to the States respectively, or to the people.

ARTICLE XI = 11th Amendment

(Proposed, 1794; Ratified, 1795)

The Judicial power of the United States shall not be construed to extend to any suit in law or equity, commenced or prosecuted against one of the United States by Citizens of another State, or by Citizens or Subjects of any Foreign State.

ARTICLE XII = 12th Amendment

(Proposed, 1803; Ratified, 1804)

The Electors shall meet in their respective states and vote by ballot for President and Vice-President, one of whom, at least, shall not be an inhabitant of the same state with themselves; they shall name in their ballots the person voted for as President, and in distinct ballots the person voted for as vice-president, and they shall make distinct lists of all persons voted for as President, and of all persons voted for as vice-president, and of the number of votes for each, which lists they shall sign and certify, and transmit sealed to the seat of the government of the United States, directed to the President of the Senate; - The President of the Senate shall, in the presence of the Senate and House of Representatives, open all the certificates and the votes shall then be counted; - The person having the greatest number of votes for President, shall be the President, if such number be a majority of the whole number of Electors appointed; and if no person have such majority, then from the persons having the highest numbers not exceeding three on the list of those voted for as President, the House of Representatives shall choose immediately, by ballot, the President. But in choosing the President, the votes shall be taken by states, the representation from each state having one vote; a quorum for this purpose shall consist of a member or members from two-thirds of the states, and a majority of all the states shall be necessary to a choice. And if the House of Representatives shall not choose a President whenever the right of choice shall devolve upon them, before the fourth day of March next following, then the vice-president shall act as President, as in the case of the death or other constitutional disability of the President. - The

person having the greatest number of votes as vice-president, shall be the vice-president, if such number be a majority of the whole number of Electors appointed, and if no person have a majority, then from the two highest numbers on the list, the Senate shall choose the vice-president; a quorum for the purpose shall consist of two-thirds of the whole number of Senators, and a majority of the whole number shall be necessary to a choice. But no person constitutionally ineligible to the office of President shall be eligible to that of vice-president of the United States.

ARTICLE XIII = 13th Amendment

(Proposed, 1865; Ratified, 1865)

Section 1. Neither slavery nor involuntary servitude, except as a punishment for crime whereof the party shall have been duly convicted, shall exist within the United States, or any place subject to their jurisdiction.

Section 2. Congress shall have power to enforce this article by appropriate legislation.

ARTICLE XIV = 14th Amendment

(Proposed, 1866; Ratified, 1868)

Section 1. All persons born or naturalized in the United States, and subject to the jurisdiction thereof, are citizens of the United States and of the State wherein they reside. No State shall make or enforce any law which shall abridge the privileges or immunities of citizens of the United States; nor shall any State deprive any person of life, liberty, or property, without due process of law; nor deny to any person within its jurisdiction the equal protection of the laws.

Section 2. Representatives shall be apportioned among the several States according to their respective numbers, counting the whole number of persons in each State, excluding Indians not taxed. But when the right to vote at any election for the choice of electors for President and Vice President of the United States, Representatives in Congress, the Executive and Judicial officers of a State, or the members of the Legislature thereof, is denied to any of the male inhabitants of such State, being twenty-one years of age, and citizens of the United States, or in any way abridged, except for participation in rebellion, or other crime, the basis of representation therein shall be reduced in the proportion which the number of such male citizens shall bear to the whole number of male citizens twenty-one years of age in such State.

Section 3. No person shall be a Senator or Representative in Congress, or elector of President and Vice President, or hold any office, civil or military, under the United States, or under any State, who, having previously taken an oath, as a member of Congress, or as an officer of the United States, or as a member of any State legislature, or as an executive or judicial officer of any State, to support the Constitution of the United States, shall have engaged in insurrection or rebellion against the same, or given aid or comfort to the enemies thereof. But Congress may by a vote of two-thirds of each House, remove such disability.

Section 4. The validity of the public debt of the United States, authorized by law, including debts incurred for payment of pensions and bounties for services in suppressing insurrection or rebellion, shall not be questioned. But neither the United States nor any State shall assume or pay any debt or obligation incurred in aid of insurrection or rebellion against the United States, or any claim for the loss or emancipation of any slave; but all such debts, obligations and claims shall be held illegal and void.

Section 5. The Congress shall have power to enforce, by appropriate legislation, the provisions of this article.

ARTICLE XV = 15th Amendment

(Proposed, 1869; Ratified, 1870)

Section 1. The right of citizens of the United States to vote shall not be denied or abridged by the United States or by any State on account of race, color, or previous condition of servitude.

Section 2. The Congress shall have power to enforce this article by appropriate legislation.

ARTICLE XVI = 16th Amendment

(Proposed, 1909; Ratified, 1913)

The Congress shall have power to lay and collect taxes on incomes, from whatever source derived, without apportionment among the several States, and without regard to any census or enumeration.

ARTICLE XVII = 17th Amendment

(Proposed, 1912; Ratified, 1913)

Par. (1) The Senate of the United States shall be composed of two Senators from each State, elected by the people thereof for six years; and each Senator shall have one vote. The electors in each State shall have the qualifications requisite for electors of the most numerous branch of the State legislatures.

Par. (2) When vacancies happen in the representation of any State in the Senate, the executive authority of such State shall issue writs of election to fill such vacancies: *Provided,* That the legislature of any State may empower the executive thereof to make temporary appointments until the people fill the vacancies by election as the legislature may direct.

Par. (3) This amendment shall not be so construed as to affect the election or term of any Senator chosen before it becomes valid as part of the Constitution.

ARTICLE XVIII = 18th Amendment

(Ratified, 1919; Repealed, 1933, by the 21st Amendment)

Section 1. After one year from the ratification of this article the manufacture, sale, or transportation of intoxicating liquors within, the importation thereof into, or the exportation thereof from the United States and all territory subject to the jurisdiction thereof for beverage purposes is hereby prohibited.

Section 2. The Congress and the several States shall have concurrent power to enforce this article by appropriate legislation.

Section 3. This article shall be inoperative unless it shall have been ratified as an amendment to the Constitution by the legislatures of the several States as provided in the Constitution, within seven years from the date of the submission hereof to the States by the Congress.

ARTICLE XIX = 19th Amendment

(Proposed, 1919; Ratified, 1920)

The right of citizens of the United States to vote shall not be denied or abridged by the United States or by any State on account of sex.

Congress shall have power to enforce this article by appropriate legislation.

ARTICLE XX = 20th Amendment

(Proposed, 1932; Ratified, 1933)

Section 1. The terms of the President and Vice President shall end at noon on the 20th day of January, and the terms of Senators and Representatives at noon on the 3rd day of January, of the years in which such terms would have ended if this article had not been ratified; and the terms of their successors shall then begin.

Section 2. The Congress shall assemble at least once in every year, and such meeting shall begin at noon on the 3rd day of January, unless they shall by law appoint a different day.

Section 3. If, at the time fixed for the beginning of the term of the President, the President elect shall have died, the Vice President elect shall become President. If a President shall not have been chosen before the time fixed for the beginning of his term, or if the President elect shall have failed to qualify, then the Vice President elect shall act as President until a President shall have qualified; and the Congress may by law provide for the case wherein neither a President elect nor a Vice President elect shall have qualified, declaring who shall then act as President, or the manner in which one who is to act shall be selected, and such person shall act accordingly until a President or Vice President shall have qualified.

Section 4. The Congress may by law provide for the case of the death of any of the persons from whom the House of Representatives may choose a President whenever the right of choice shall have devolved upon them, and for the case of the death of any of the persons from whom the Senate may choose a Vice President whenever the right of choice shall have devolved upon them.

Section 5. Sections 1 and 2 shall take effect on the 15th day of October following the ratification of this article.

Section 6. This article shall be inoperative unless it shall have been ratified as an amendment to the Constitution by the legislatures of three-fourths of the several States within seven years from the date of its submission.

ARTICLE XXI = 21st Amendment

(Proposed, 1933; Ratified, 1933)

Section 1. The eighteenth article of amendment to the Constitution of the United States is hereby repealed.

Section 2. The transportation or importation into any State, Territory, or possession of the United States for delivery or use therein of intoxicating liquors, in violation of the laws thereof, is hereby prohibited.

Section 3. This article shall be inoperative unless it shall have been ratified as an amendment to the Constitution by conventions in the several States, as provided in the Constitution, within seven years from the date of the submission hereof to the States by the Congress.

ARTICLE XXII = 22nd Amendment

(Proposed, 1947; Ratified, 1951)

Section 1. No person shall be elected to the office of the President more than twice, and no person who has held the office of President, or acted as President, for more than two years of a term to which some other person was elected President shall be elected to the office of the President more than once. But this Article shall not apply to any person holding the office of President when this Article was proposed by the Congress, and shall not prevent any person who may be holding the office of President, or acting as President, during the term within which this Article becomes operative from holding the office of President or acting as President during the remainder of such term.

Section 2. This article shall be inoperative unless it shall have been ratified as an amendment to the Constitution by the legislatures of three-fourths of the several States within seven years from the date of its submission to the States by the Congress.

ARTICLE XXIII = 23rd Amendment

(Proposed, 1960; Ratified, 1961)

Section 1. The District constituting the seat of Government of the United States shall appoint in such manner as the Congress may direct:

A number of electors of President and Vice President equal to the whole number of Senators and Representatives in Congress to which the District would be entitled if it were a State, but in no event more than the least populous State; they shall be in addition to those appointed by the States, but they shall be considered, for the purposes of the election of President and Vice President, to be electors appointed by a State; and they shall meet in the District and perform such duties as provided by the twelfth article of amendment.

Section 2. The Congress shall have power to enforce this article by appropriate legislation.

ARTICLE XXIV = 24th Amendment

(Proposed, 1962; Ratified, 1964)

Section 1. The right of citizens of the United States to vote in any primary or other election for President or Vice President, for electors for President or Vice President, or for Senator or Representative in Congress, shall not be denied or abridged by the United States or any State by reason of failure to pay any poll tax or other tax.

Section 2. The Congress shall have power to enforce this article by appropriate legislation.

ARTICLE XXV = 25th Amendment

(Proposed, 1965; Ratified, 1967)

Section 1. In case of the removal of the President from office or of his death or resignation, the Vice President shall become President.

Section 2. Whenever there is a vacancy in the office of the Vice President, the President shall nominate a Vice President who shall take office upon confirmation by a majority vote of both Houses of Congress.

Section 3. Whenever the President transmits to the President pro tempore of the Senate and the Speaker of the House of Representatives his written declaration that he is unable to discharge the powers and duties of his office, and until he transmits to them a written declaration to the contrary, such powers and duties shall be discharged by the Vice President as Acting President.

Section 4. Par. (1) Whenever the Vice President and a majority of either the principal officers of the executive departments or of such other body as Congress may be law provide, transmit to the President pro tempore of the Senate and the Speaker of the House of Representatives their written declaration that the President is unable to discharge the powers and duties of his office, the Vice President shall immediately assume the powers and duties of the office as Acting President.

Par. (2) Thereafter, when the President transmits to the President pro tempore of the Senate and the Speaker of the House of Representatives his written declaration that no inability exists, he shall resume the powers and duties of his office unless the Vice President and a majority of either the principal officers of the executive department or of such other body as Congress may by law provide, transmit within four days to the President pro tempore of the Senate and the Speaker of the House of Representatives their written declaration that the President is unable to discharge the powers and duties of his office. Thereupon Congress shall decide the issue, assembling within forty-eight hours for that purpose if not in session. If the Congress, within twenty-one days after receipt of the latter written declaration, or, if Congress is not in session, within twenty-one days after Congress is required to assemble, determines by two-thirds vote of both Houses that the President is unable to discharge the powers and duties of his office, the Vice President shall continue to discharge the same as Acting President; otherwise, the President shall resume the powers and duties of his office.

ARTICLE XXVI = 26th Amendment

(Proposed, 1971; Ratified, 1971)

Section 1. The right of citizens of the United States, who are eighteen years of age or older, to vote shall not be denied or abridged by the United States or by any State on account of age.

Section 2. The Congress shall have the power to enforce this article by appropriate legislation.

ARTICLE XXVII = 27th Amendment

(Proposed, 1789; Ratified, 1992)

No law, varying the compensation for the services of the Senators and Representatives shall take effect, until an election of Representatives shall have intervened.

Bibliography

Books

Ballantine, Betty and Ian Ballantine, eds. *The Native Americans*, an Illustrated History. Atlanta, GA: Turner Publishing, Inc., 1993.

Bartlett, John. *Bartlett's Familiar Quotations.* Boston: Little, Brown and Company, 1992.

Billard, Jules B., ed. *The World of the American Indian*, National Geographic Society. Washington, DC: The National Geographic Book Division, 1993.

Blassingame, Wyatt. *The Look-It-Up Book of Presidents*, Rev. Ed. New York: Random House, 1993.

Boorstin, Daniel J. *The Americans, a Trilogy: The Colonial Experience, The National Experience, The Democratic Experience.* New York: Vintage Books, A Division of Random House, 1974.

_____. *The Constitution of the United States of America.* Inscribed and Illustrated by Sam Fink. Forward by James A. Michener. New York: Random House, 1985.

Freeman, Douglas Southall. *R.E. Lee*, 4 Vols. Richard Harwell. *Lee,* Abridg. in 1 Vol. New York: Charles Scribner's Sons, 1961.

Galub, Arthur L. and George J. Lankevich. *The United States Supreme Court - The Rehnquist Court 1986-1994*, Vol. X. Danbury, CT: Grolier Educational Corp., 1995.

Hall, Kermit L., ed. *The Oxford Companion to the Supreme Court of the United States.* New York: Oxford University Press, Inc., 1992.

Hitchcock, Charles B., ed. *These United States*. Pleasantville, New York: The Reader's Digest Association, 1968.

Hitchings, Thomas E., ed. In chief. *Facts-On-File Yearbook*, 1995. Vol. LV. New York: Facts On File, Inc., 1995.

Orvedahl, Jerry A., ed. *Washington Information Directory, 1994-1995*. Washington, DC: Congressional Quarterly, Inc., 1994.

Peltason, J.W., Corwin and Peltason's *Understanding the Constitution*, 11th Ed. University of California, Irvine: The Dryden Press, Saunders College Publishing. Holt, Rinehart and Winston, Inc., 1988.

Witt, Elder, ed. Congressional Quarterly's *Guide to the U.S. Supreme Court.* Washington, DC: Congressional Quarterly Inc., 1979.

Government Publications

_____. *American Indians Today*. Pamphlet, Code 130. Bureau of Indian Affairs. Washington, DC: Department of the Interior, 1987.

Girard, Martha L., dir. *The United States Government Manual, 1994/1995*. Office of the Federal Register, National Archives and Records Administration. Lanham, MD: Bernan Press, 1994.

_____. "The Indian Tribes, a Continuing Quest For Survival." *Report of the U.S. Commission on Civil Rights*, June 1981. Permit No. G73. Washington, DC: U.S. Government Printing Office, 1981.

Jayson, Lester S. sup. ed. *The Constitution of the United States of America*. Prepared by the Congressional Research Service Library of Congress. Washington DC: Government Printing Office, 1973.

Mason, Leslie and Duane Nystrom, eds. *1993-1994 Congressional Directory, 103rd Congress*. Joint Committee on Printing, U.S. Congress. Lanham, MD: Bernan Press, 1993.

Tyler, S. Lyman. *A History of Indian Policy*. Stock No. 2402-00031. United States Department of the Interior, Bureau of Indian Affairs. Washington, DC: U.S. Government Printing Office, 1973.

_____. *United States Code*, 1988 Ed. Supplement V, Vol. 4. Titles 20-25, January 3, 1989 to January 24, 1994: General and Permanent Laws of the United States Enacted During the 101st, 102nd and 103rd Congress,

First Session. Washington, DC: United States Government Printing Office.

MISCELLANEOUS

Editors of Time. *Time Annual, 1995 - The Year in Review:* New York: Time Inc. 1996.

Famighetti, Robert, ed. *The World Almanac and Book of Facts*, 1995 and 1996 Eds. Mahwah, NJ: World Almanac, Imprint of Funk and Wagnals Corp., 1995, 1996

Johnson, Otto, exec. ed. 1995 and 1996 *Information Please Almanac - Atlas and Yearbook,* 48th and 49th Eds. Boston and New York: Houghton Mifflin Co., 1995, 1996

_____. "Justice For Women__" Ruth Bader Ginsburg. *Vogue*, magazine, October, 1993. Beverly Hills, California: The Condé Nast Publications, Inc., 1993.

Levy, Leonard W., ed. *Encyclopedia of the American Constitution.* Vols. 1-4, 1986. Supplement 1, 1992 Ed. New York: MacMillan Publishing Company, 1992.

_____. *Newsweek*, magazine. Special Election Issue November/December, 1992. Vol. CXX, No. 27. New York: Newsweek, Inc., 1992.

_____. "The Practical Idealist - Stephen Breyer." *The Washington Post*, weekly newspaper. Vol. 2, No. 36, July 4-10, 1994.

Smoke, Stephen D., ed. Case Study No. 1, "Bible Reading and Prayer in Public Schools - The Schempp Case." Supreme Court decision: *Schempp v Pennsylvania (1963*). "Verdict" insert in *Social Education*, magazine of the National Council of the Social Studies. Washington, DC: Department of Social Education, 1964.

_____. *The World Book Encyclopedia*. Chicago: World Book, Inc., 1993.

_____. *Time*, magazine. Election Special. November 18, 1996 Vol. 148, No. 23. New York: Time Inc., 1996.

_____. *U.S. News & World Report*, magazine. June 5, 1995 issue. Vol. 118, No. 22. Washington, DC: U.S. News & World Report, Inc., 1995.

Person to Person

Dooley, Dr. Thomas A. Never-to-be-forgotten deceased personal friend. Autobiography: *Deliver Us From Evil*. The Vietnam transition period from French to American involvement in which Dr. Dooley secured health and safety for hundreds of thousands of refugees fleeing North Vietnam. Forward by Admiral Arleigh Burke, Chief of Naval Operations, U.S. Navy. New York: Farrar, Strauss and Company, 1956.

Merkle, Robert B., of New Smyrna Beach, Florida and Waynesville, North Carolina. Former U.S. Army helicopter pilot. One tour of duty, Korean War and two tours of duty, Vietnam War. Interview: Waynesville, North Carolina, October, 1994.

Paul, Wilbur, Cherokee Superintendent of the Bureau of Indian Affairs, and Jonathan L. Taylor, Cherokee Chief. Interviews: their Cherokee homeland, the Great Smoky Mountains of Western North Carolina, August, 1993.

Subject Index

B

C

D

E